Morning Madness May 27-30

Lunch Count/Back packs, Folders/Attendance

Opening Task / Pledge of Allegiance *Español*

Open Court Whole Group

CCSS.ELA-Literacy.RL.2.1 Ask and answer such questions as *who, what, where, when, why,* and *how* to demonstrate understanding of key details in a text. CCSS.ELA-Literacy.RL.2.2 Recount stories, including fables and folktales from diverse cultures, and determine their central message, lesson, or moral.CCSS.ELA-Literacy.RL.2.3 Describe how characters in a story respond to major events and challenges.CCSS.ELA-Literacy.RL.3.1 Ask and answer questions to demonstrate understanding of a text, referring explicitly to the text as the basis for the answers.CCSS.ELA-Literacy.RL.3.2 Recount stories, including fables, folktales, and myths from diverse cultures; determine the central message, lesson, or moral and explain how it is conveyed through key details in the text.CCSS.ELA-Literacy.RL.3.3 Describe characters in a story (e.g., their traits, motivations, or feelings) and explain how their actions contribute to the sequence of events

Dinero /Un abrigo para ANNA/ Bumping, Combination Dictation-CIA, Setting Connection Thinking MAP, introduce spelling high frequency words 4.5/4.4, Vocab. /fluency

Centers

Gle K 2.21, 2.41, 3.21, Wr 1.11, Wr 1.41, 2.41

ABC's / Drama/ Vocabulary /Teacher Guided / Books/ Listening/ Fluency

Walk to RECESS- LUNCH @ 11:45-12:20

Freestyle dance
CIA- Read Aloud "La Isla de los delfines"

Handwriting Without Tears

Multimedia-Mon@ 1:20 Biblioteca -Tues@10:25
PE Wed@9:15 Musica- Thur@10:25

PE-Fri@10:25

Writing Workshop Books / Native Americans

CCSS.ELA-Literacy.W.2.1 Write opinion pieces in which they introduce the topic or book they are writing about, state an opinion, supply reasons that support the opinion, use linking words (e.g., *because, and, also*) to connect opinion and reasons, and provide a concluding statement or section.CCSS.ELA-Literacy.W.2.2 Write informative/explanatory texts in which they introduce a topic, use facts and definitions to develop points, and provide a concluding statement or section.CCSS.ELA-Literacy.W.2.3 Write narratives in which they recount a well-elaborated event or short sequence of events, include details to describe actions, thoughts, and feelings, use temporal words to signal event order, and provide a sense of closure.CCSS.ELA-Literacy.W.3.1a Introduce the topic or text they are writing about, state an opinion, and create an organizational structure that lists reasons.CCSS.ELA-Literacy.W.3.1b Provide reasons that support the opinion.CCSS.ELA-Literacy.W.3.1c Use linking words and phrases (e.g., *because, therefore, since, for example*) to connect opinion and reasons.CCSS.ELA-Literacy.W.3.1d Provide a concluding statement or section.

Recreo @ 1:55

Social Studies, Native Americans –/OBLAH DI / Science

Matemáticas

CCSS.Math.Content.2.OA.A.1 Use addition and subtraction within 100 to solve one- and two-step word problems involving situations of adding to, taking from, putting together, taking apart, and comparing, with unknowns in all positions, e.g., by using drawings and equations with a symbol for the unknown number to represent the problem.[1]CCSS.Math.Content.2.OA.B.2 Fluently add and subtract within 20 using mental strategies.[2] By end of Grade 2, know from memory all sums of two one-digit numbers. CCSS.Math.Content.3.OA.A.1 Interpret products of whole numbers, e.g., interpret 5 × 7 as the total number of objects in 5 groups of 7 objects each. *For example, describe a context in which a total number of objects can be expressed as 5 × 7.* CCSS.Math.Content.3.OA.A.3 Use multiplication and division within 100 to solve word problems in situations involving equal groups, arrays, and measurement quantities, e.g., by using drawings and equations with a symbol for the unknown number to represent the problem.[1]

Resolver, Fact Masters, Matemáticas En contacto/ Kems

Math Connects 2/3, IXl, , Multiplication, Fractions, Addition

Centros Shapes, numbers 0-100, Legos, puzzles, books, Adding and Multiplication Chutes and ladders, bingo, Measuring/ ipods, IXL, 10X

Calendario-Planners

Closing Procedures Folder/Chairs/ Back Packs

Adios

Morning Madness May 27-30

Lunch Count/Back packs, Folders/Attendance

Opening Task / Pledge of Allegiance *Español*

Open Court Whole Group

CCSS.ELA-Literacy.RL.2.1 Ask and answer such questions as *who, what, where, when, why,* and *how* to demonstrate understanding of key details in a text. CCSS.ELA-Literacy.RL.2.2 Recount stories, including fables and folktales from diverse cultures, and determine their central message, lesson, or moral. CCSS.ELA-Literacy.RL.2.3 Describe how characters in a story respond to major events and challenges. CCSS.ELA-Literacy.RL.3.1 Ask and answer questions to demonstrate understanding of a text, referring explicitly to the text as the basis for the answers. CCSS.ELA-Literacy.RL.3.2 Recount stories, including fables, folktales, and myths from diverse cultures; determine the central message, lesson, or moral and explain how it is conveyed through key details in the text. CCSS.ELA-Literacy.RL.3.3 Describe characters in a story (e.g., their traits, motivations, or feelings) and explain how their actions contribute to the sequence of events

Dinero /Un abrigo para ANNA/ Bumping, Combination Dictation-CIA, Setting Connection Thinking MAP, introduce spelling high frequency words 4.5/4.4, Vocab. /fluency

Centers

Gle K 2.21, 2.41, 3.21, wr 1.11, wr 1.41, 2.41

ABC's / Drama/ Vocabulary /Teacher Guided / Books/ Listening/ Fluency

Walk to RECESS- LUNCH @ 11:45-12:20

Freestyle dance
CIA- Read Aloud "La Isla de los delfines"

Handwriting Without Tears

Multimedia-Mon@ 1:20 Biblioteca -Tues@10:25
PE Wed@9:15 Musica- Thur@10:25

PE-Fri@10:25

Writing Workshop Books / Native Americans

CCSS.ELA-Literacy.W.2.1 Write opinion pieces in which they introduce the topic or book they are writing about, state an opinion, supply reasons that support the opinion, use linking words (e.g., *because, and, also*) to connect opinion and reasons, and provide a concluding statement or section.CCSS.ELA-Literacy.W.2.2 Write informative/explanatory texts in which they introduce a topic, use facts and definitions to develop points, and provide a concluding statement or section.CCSS.ELA-Literacy.W.2.3 Write narratives in which they recount a well-elaborated event or short sequence of events, include details to describe actions, thoughts, and feelings, use temporal words to signal event order, and provide a sense of closure.CCSS.ELA-Literacy.W.3.1a Introduce the topic or text they are writing about, state an opinion, and create an organizational structure that lists reasons.CCSS.ELA-Literacy.W.3.1b Provide reasons that support the opinion.CCSS.ELA-Literacy.W.3.1c Use linking words and phrases (e.g., *because, therefore, since, for example*) to connect opinion and reasons.CCSS.ELA-Literacy.W.3.1d Provide a concluding statement or section.

Recreo @ 1:55

Social Studies, Native Americans –/OBLAH DI / Science

Matemáticas

CCSS.Math.Content.2.OA.A.1 Use addition and subtraction within 100 to solve one- and two-step word problems involving situations of adding to, taking from, putting together, taking apart, and comparing, with unknowns in all positions, e.g., by using drawings and equations with a symbol for the unknown number to represent the problem.[1]CCSS.Math.Content.2.OA.B.2 Fluently add and subtract within 20 using mental strategies.[2] By end of Grade 2, know from memory all sums of two one-digit numbers. CCSS.Math.Content.3.OA.A.1 Interpret products of whole numbers, e.g., interpret 5 × 7 as the total number of objects in 5 groups of 7 objects each. *For example, describe a context in which a total number of objects can be expressed as 5 × 7.* CCSS.Math.Content.3.OA.A.3 Use multiplication and division within 100 to solve word problems in situations involving equal groups, arrays, and measurement quantities, e.g., by using drawings and equations with a symbol for the unknown number to represent the problem.[1]

Resolver, Fact Masters, Matemáticas En contacto/ Kems

Math Connects 2/3, IXl, , Multiplication, Fractions, Addition

Centros Shapes, numbers 0-100, Legos, puzzles, books, Adding and Multiplication Chutes and ladders, bingo, Measuring/ ipods, IXL, 10X

Calendario-Planners

Closing Procedures Folder/Chairs/ Back Packs

Adios

Student Workbook

Show What You Know® on the
MSP

3

**Preparation for the Measurements of Student Progress
Washington Comprehensive Assessment Program**

Name: _____

Published by:

Show What You Know® Publishing
www.ShowWhatYouKnowPublishing.com

Distributed by:
Lorenz Educational Press, a Lorenz company
P.O. Box 802
Dayton, OH 45401-0802
www.LorenzEducationalPress.com

Copyright © 2009 by Show What You Know® Publishing
All rights reserved.

No part of this book, including interior design, cover design, and icons, may be reproduced or transmitted in any form, by any means (electronic, photocopying, recording, or otherwise).

Standards are from the Common Core State Standards Initiative Web site at www.corestandards.org dated 2011.

Printed in the United States of America

ISBN: 978-1-5923-0336-6

Limit of Liability/Disclaimer of Warranty: The authors and publishers have used their best efforts in preparing this book. Show What You Know® Publishing and the authors make no representations or warranties with respect to the contents of this book and specifically disclaim any implied warranties and shall in no event be liable for any loss of any kind including but not limited to special, incidental, consequential, or other damages.

Acknowledgements

Show What You Know® Publishing acknowledges the following for their efforts in making this assessment material available for Washington students, parents, and teachers:

Cindi Englefield, President/Publisher
Eloise Boehm-Sasala, Vice President/Managing Editor
Christine Filippetti, Production Editor
Jill Borish, Production Editor
Jennifer Harney, Editor/Illustrator

About the Contributors

The content of this book was written BY teachers FOR teachers and students and was designed specifically for the Measurements of Student Progress (MSP) for Grade 3. Contributions to the Reading and Mathematics sections of this book were also made by the educational publishing staff at Show What You Know® Publishing. Dr. Jolie S. Brams, a clinical child and family psychologist, is the contributing author of the Worry Less About Tests and Test-Taking Hints for Test Heroes chapters of this book. Without the contributions of these people, this book would not be possible.

Table of Contents

Introduction v

Worry Less About Tests 1

Test-Taking Hints for Test Heroes 9

Reading 21
    Introduction 21
    About the Reading MSP 22
        Item Distribution 22
        Scoring 23
    Glossary of Reading Terms 24
    Reading Practice Tutorial 27
    Directions 28
    Reading Assessment One 43
    Reading Assessment Two 67

Mathematics 95
    Introduction 95
    About the Mathematics MSP 96
        Item Distribution 96
        Scoring 96
    Glossary of Mathematics Terms 97
    Glossary of Mathematics Illustrations 105
    Mathematics Practice Tutorial 111
    Directions 112
    Mathematics Assessment 147

Introduction

Dear Student:

This *Show What You Know® on the MSP for Grade 3, Student Workbook* was created to give you lots of practice in preparation for the Measurements of Student Progress (MSP) in Reading and Mathematics.

The first two chapters in this workbook—Worry Less About Tests and Test-Taking Hints for Test Heroes—were written especially for third-grade students. Worry Less About Tests offers advice on how to get rid of the bad feelings you may have about tests. The Test-Taking Hints for Test Heroes chapter gives you examples of the kinds of questions you will see on the MSP, such as multiple-choice and short-answer, and includes helpful tips on how to answer these questions correctly so you can succeed on the MSP.

The next two chapters of this Student Workbook help you prepare for the Reading and Mathematics MSP.
- The Reading chapter includes a Reading Practice Tutorial, two full-length Reading Assessments, and a Reading Glossary of words that will help you show what you know on the MSP.
- The Mathematics chapter includes a Mathematics Practice Tutorial, a full-length Mathematics Assessment, a Glossary of Mathematics Terms, and a Glossary of Mathematical Illustrations that will help you show what you know on the MSP.

This Student Workbook will help you become familiar with the look and feel of the MSP and will provide a chance to practice your test-taking skills to show what you know.

Good luck on the MSP!

This page intentionally left blank.

Worry Less About Tests

Introduction

Many of us get nervous or anxious before taking a test. We want to do our best, and we worry that we might fail. You may have heard of the Measurements of Student Progress (MSP), although you may not be familiar with the actual MSP assessment. Because the MSP is new to you, you may become scared. You may worry about the test, and this might interfere with your ability to show what you know.

This chapter offers tips you can use on the MSP and many other tests. The ideas will build your test-taking confidence.

Worry Less About Tests

There are many things most of us would rather do than take a test. What would you rather do? Go to recess? See a movie? Eat a snack? Go swimming? Take a test? Most of us would not choose take a test. This doesn't mean we're afraid of tests. It means we like to do things that are more fun!

Some students do not want to take tests for another reason. They are afraid of tests and are afraid of failing. Even though they are smart enough to do well, they are scared. All of us worry about a test at one time or another. So, if you worry about tests, you are not alone.

When people worry about tests or are scared of tests, they have what is called test stress. You may have heard your parents say, "I'm feeling really stressed today." That means they have worried feelings. These feelings of stress can get in the way of doing your best. When you have test stress, it will be harder to show what you know. This chapter will help you get over your stress and worry less. You won't be scared. You will feel calm, happy, and proud.

If your mind is a mess
Because of terrible stress,
And you feel that you can't change at all.
Just pick up this book,
And take a look,
Our tips won't let you fall!

It's OK to Worry a Little Bit

Most people worry a little bit about something. Worrying isn't always a bad thing. A small amount of worrying is helpful. If you worry about crossing the street, you are more careful. When you worry about your school work, you work hard to do it right. As you can see, a little worrying isn't bad. However, you have to make sure you don't let worrying get in the way of doing your best. Think about crossing the street. If you worry too much, you'll never go anywhere. You can see how worrying too much is not a good thing.

Third graders have a very special job. That job is taking the MSP. The people who give the MSP want to know what you're learning in school. MSP stands for Measurements of Student Progress. All children in Washington are terrific and can learn to do their best on the MSP without worrying too much or too little.

What Kind of Kid Are You?

Test stress and worrying too much or too little can get in your way. The good news is there are ways you can help yourself do better on tests. All you have to do is change the way you think about taking tests. You can do better, not just by learning more or studying more, but by changing the way you think about things.

Now you will read about some students who changed the way they think about tests. You may see that these students have some of the same feelings you have. You will learn how each of these kids faced a problem and ended up doing better on tests.

Stay-Away Stephanie
Stephanie thought that it was better to stay away from tests than to try at all. She was scared to face tests. She thought, "If I stay home sick, I won't have to take the test. I don't care if I get in trouble; I'm just not going to take the test." Stay-Away Stephanie felt less nervous when she ran away from tests, but she never learned to face her fear. Stephanie's teacher thought Stephanie didn't care about tests or school, but this wasn't true at all. Stay-Away Stephanie really worried about tests. She stayed away instead of trying to face each challenge.

One day, Stephanie's mom had an idea! "Stephanie, do you remember when you were afraid to ride your bike after I took the training wheels off?" her mom said. "You would hide whenever I wanted to take a bike ride. You said, 'I would rather walk than learn to ride a two-wheel bike.'" Stephanie knew that wasn't true. She wanted to learn to ride her bike, but she was scared. She stayed away from the challenge. When Stephanie faced her fear, step by step, she learned to ride her bike. "Stephanie," her mom said, "I think you stay away from tests because you're worried." Stephanie knew her mom was right. She had to face tests step by step.

Stephanie and her teacher came up with a plan. First, Stephanie's teacher gave her two test questions to do in school. For homework, Stephanie did two more questions. When Stephanie was scared, she talked with her mom or her teacher. She didn't stay away. Soon, Stephanie knew how to ask for help, and she took tests without being worried. Now, she has a new nickname: Super-Successful Stephanie!

If you are like Stay-Away Stephanie, talk with your teacher or someone who can help you. Together, you can learn to take tests one step at a time. You will be a successful student instead of a stay-away student.

Worried Wendy

Wendy always thought that the worst would happen. Her mind worried about everything. "What if I can't answer all the questions? What if I don't do well? My teacher won't like me. My dad will be upset. I will have to study a lot more." Wendy spent her time worrying. Instead, she should have learned to do well on tests.

Wendy was so worried her stomach hurt. Wendy's doctor knew she wasn't sick; she was worried. "Wendy," he said, "I have known you ever since you were born. You have always been curious. You wanted to know how everything worked and where everything was. But now your curious mind is playing tricks on you. You are so worried, you're making yourself sick."

Wendy's doctor put a clock on his desk. "Look at this clock. Is it a good clock or a bad clock?" Wendy had no answer. "Believe it or not, Wendy, we can trick our minds into thinking it is good or bad. I'm going to say bad things about this clock as fast as I can. First, it's not very big. Also, because the clock is small, I might not read the time on it correctly. Since the clock is so small, I might lose it forever." Wendy agreed it was a bad clock. "But wait," said her doctor. "I think the clock is a neat shape, and I like the colors. I like having it in my office; it tells time well. It didn't cost much, so if I lose it, it isn't a big deal." Wendy realized she could look at tests the way the doctor looked at the clock. You don't have to worry. You can see good things, not bad.

Critical Carlos

Carlos always put himself down. He thought he failed at everything he did. If he got a B+ on his homework, he would say, "I made so many mistakes, I didn't get an A." He never said good things like, "I worked hard. I'm proud of my B+." Carlos didn't do well on tests because he told himself, "I don't do well on anything, especially tests."

Last week, Carlos got a 95% on a test about lakes and rivers. Carlos stared at his paper. He was upset. "What is the matter, Carlos?" his teacher asked. "Is something wrong?" Carlos replied, "I'm stupid; I missed five points. I should have gotten a 100%."

"Carlos, nobody's perfect: not me, not you, not anybody. I think 95 out of 100 is super! It's not perfect, but it is very good. Celebrate, Carlos!" Carlos smiled; he knew his teacher was right. Now, Carlos knows he has to feel good about what he does. He isn't sad about his mistakes. He's cheerful, not critical.

Look at the chart below. Use this chart to find out all the good things about yourself. Some examples are given to get you started.

Good Things About Me

1. *I make my grandmother happy when I tell her a joke.*

2. *I taught my dog how to shake hands.*

3. *I can do two somersaults in a row.*

4.

5.

6.

Victim Vince

Vince couldn't take responsibility for himself. He said everything was someone else's fault. "The MSP is too hard. I won't do well because they made the test too hard. And, last night, my little brother made so much noise that I couldn't write my homework story. It's his fault I won't do well. I asked Mom to buy my favorite snack. I have to have it when I study. She forgot to pick it up at the store. I can't study without my snack. It's her fault." Vince complained and complained.

Vince's aunt told him he had to stop blaming everyone for his troubles. "You can make a difference, Vince," she said. "When is your next test?" Vince told her he had a spelling test on Friday. "You're going to be the boss of the test. First, let's pick a time to study. How is every day at 4:00 p.m.?" Vince agreed. "Now, how are you going to study?"

"I like to practice writing the words a couple of times," Vince said. "Then, I ask Mom or Dad to quiz me."

"Great idea. Every day at 4:00 p.m., you're going to write each word four times. Then, ask one of your parents to review your list. You're the boss of the spelling test, Vince, because you have a plan."

Vince's Study Plan

TIME	Monday	Tuesday	Wednesday	Thursday	Friday
					Spelling Test!
4:00	Write down spelling words. Then, ask Mom or Dad to help.	Write down spelling words. Then, ask Mom or Dad to help.	Write down spelling words. Then, ask Mom or Dad to help.	Write down spelling words. Then, ask Mom or Dad to help.	
4:30					
5:00					
5:30					
6:00					
7:00	Look at spelling words again.	Look at spelling words again.	Look at spelling words again.	Look at spelling words again.	
7:30					Get a movie for doing well!

When Friday came, Vince's whole world changed. Instead of being in a bad mood because of a poor grade, Vince felt powerful! He took his spelling test and scored an A-. Vince could not believe his eyes! His teacher was thrilled. Vince soon learned he could control his attitude. Vince is no longer a victim. Instead, he is Victor Vince.

Perfect Pat

Pat spent all her time studying. She told herself, "I **should** study more. I **should** write this book report over. I **should** study every minute for the MSP." Trying hard is fine, but Pat worked so much, she never felt she had done enough. Pat always thought she should be studying. Pat would play with her friends, but she never had a good time. In the middle of kickball or crafts, Pat thought, "I should be preparing for the MSP. I should be writing my book report." When Pat took a test, she worried about each question. "I can't answer this one. I should have studied harder."

"Pat," her principal said, "you have to relax. You're not enjoying school." Pat replied, "I can't do that. There is so much more to learn." The principal gave Pat some tips on how to use her study time better.

- Do not study for long periods of time. Instead, try to work for about 10–20 minutes at a time, and then take a break. Everyone needs a break!

- Ask yourself questions as you go along. After you study a fact, test yourself to see if you remember it. As you read, ask yourself questions about what you are reading. Think about what you are studying!

- Find a special time to study. You may want to think of a good time to study with the help of your parents or your teacher. You could choose to study from 4:30 to 5:00 every day after school. After dinner, you could work from 7:30 to 8:00. After you finish studying, do not worry! You have done a lot for a third grader.

- Remember, you are a third-grade kid! School is very important, but playing, having fun, and being with your friends and family are also very important parts of growing up. Having fun does not mean you won't do well in school. It doesn't mean you will do poorly on the MSP either. Having fun in your life makes you a happier person and helps you do better on tests.

"Everyone Else Is Better" Edward
Edward worried about everyone else. During holidays, Edward thought about the presents other people received. At his baseball game, he worried his teammates would score more runs. Edward always wanted to know how his friends did on tests. He spent so much time worrying about what other people were doing, he forgot to pay attention to his own studying and test taking.

"Edward, you're not going to succeed if you don't worry about yourself," his grandfather told him. "You need to start talking about what **you** can do. Instead of asking your friend how he did on a test, you say, 'I got an 85%. Next time, I want to get a 90%.'" When Edward practiced this, he worried less about tests and was a whole lot happier.

Shaky Sam

Sam was great at sports. He was friendly and funny, and he had many friends. However, Sam had one big problem. Every time he thought about taking a test, he would start shaking inside. His heart would start pounding like a drum. His stomach would get upset. Even the night before a test, he started shaking really hard.

Sam's older brother liked to sing. He told Sam he used to get nervous before he sang to a crowd of people. "Sam, you need to trick your body. Don't think about the test; think about something fun and happy."

Sam closed his eyes. He thought about making four shots in a row on the basketball court. He thought about his favorite dessert: vanilla ice cream. He thought about swimming in his neighbor's pool. When he opened his eyes, he wasn't shaking.

Practice thinking happy thoughts, and make believe you are far away from your troubles. Test stress will disappear.

Other Ways That Third Graders Have Stopped Worrying About Tests

Third graders are pretty smart kids. They have lots of good ideas for getting rid of test stress. Here are some ideas from other third graders.

- When I am scared or worried, I talk to my neighbor. She is 70 years old. She is the smartest person I know. We sit on her porch and eat cookies and talk. It makes me feel better to know that she had some of the same problems when she was in third grade. She did well in school, and I know I can, too.
- Everything is harder in third grade, especially reading and math. I didn't want to go to school. I talked to my teacher, and he said we should have a talk every day before class. We talk about my homework, and he gives me tips. This really calms me down. When I am calm, I always do better.
- I used to worry that I wasn't doing well in school. I thought everyone else was smarter. My dad gave me a special folder. I keep all my tests in it. When I look at the tests, I see how much I have learned. I know I am doing a good job.

Washington kids are smart kids! You, your teachers, and your family and friends can help you find other ways to beat test stress. You will be surprised how much you know and how well you will do on the MSP.

Test-Taking Hints for Test Heroes

Introduction

Many third graders have not seen a test like the MSP on which they have to fill in answer bubbles or write answers on lines. Before you sit down to take a test, it is a good idea to review problem-solving and test-taking hints.

This chapter offers many hints you can use when you take the MSP and other tests. The ideas will build your confidence and improve your test-taking skills.

Do Your Best on the MSP: Think Like a Genius!

Most third graders think the smartest kids do the best on tests. Smart kids may do well on tests, but all kids can do their best. By learning some helpful hints, most kids can do better than they ever thought they could on tests.

Learning to do well on tests will be helpful to you throughout your whole life, not just in third grade. Kids who are test smart feel very good about themselves. They have an "I can do it" feeling about themselves. This feeling helps them succeed in school, in sports, and in music. It even helps with making friends. Test-smart kids usually do well in their school work, too. They believe they can do anything.

Become an Awesome Test Hero!

1. Fill In the Answer Bubble

You will use a pencil to take the MSP. Think about tests you have taken. To answer questions, you may have written an answer, circled the correct answer, or solved a math problem. The MSP is different. You will use your pencil to fill in answer bubbles. The test is mostly multiple choice, but there are a few short-answer questions for which you will write your answers on lines.

For each multiple-choice question, you will have three choices to pick from. After you read the question and all the answer choices, think about which choice is correct. Next to each choice, you will see an answer bubble. The answer bubbles are not very big. They are smaller than the end of an eraser, smaller than a dime, and smaller than a jellybean. Even though the answer bubbles are small, they are very important. To answer each question, you must fill in the answer bubble next to the correct choice. Only fill in one answer bubble for each multiple-choice question. Fill in the bubble all the way, and do not color outside the bubble. Make sure you fill in the answer bubble neatly when you take the MSP.

Look at the example below. You can see the correct way to fill in an answer bubble. Practice filling in the answer bubbles in this example.

There was a girl named Devine,
Who thought that a dot was a line!
She didn't fill in the bubble;
She was really in trouble!
When her answers are wrong she will whine!

Correct: ●   Incorrect:

Practice filling in the answer bubbles here: ○ ○ ○ ○ ○ ○

Learning how to fill in answer bubbles takes practice, practice, and more practice! It may not be how you are used to marking the correct answer, but it is one way to give a right answer on the MSP. Think about Kay!

A stubborn girl named Kay,
Liked to answer questions her own way.
So her marked answer bubbles,
Gave her all sorts of troubles.
Her test scores ruined her day!

You will also have to answer short-answer questions. These are questions for which you have to write the answer. Some questions will only require one or two words or short phrases, but other questions may require a full sentence or two. Remember to write clearly and neatly so that people can read what you have written. Correct spelling and proper grammar will help to make your response clear. However, if you misspell a word or forget to use a comma or period, it will *not* be counted against you. The most important thing to remember when you answer short-answer questions is to completely answer the question as best you can.

2. Only Fill In the Answer Bubbles You Need To

It is not a good idea to touch the answer bubbles with your pencil until you are ready to fill in the right answer. If you put marks on more than one answer bubble, the computer that grades your test won't know which choice you think is right. Sometimes, kids get a little worried during the test. They might play with their pencils and tap their answer booklets. This is not a good idea. Look at all the answer choices. Only fill in one answer bubble for each multiple-choice question. This should be the answer bubble for the choice you think is right. Do not put marks in any other answer bubbles.

There was a nice girl named Sue,
Who thought she knew what to do.
She marked all the spots.
Her paper was covered with dots!
And she didn't show all that she knew.

3. Think Good Thoughts

The better you feel about taking tests, the better you will do. Imagine you are a famous sports hero. You feel good about playing your favorite sport. You feel good about yourself. As a sports hero, you don't start a soccer game, football game, baseball game, tennis match, or swimming meet by saying, "This is going to be hard. I can't do it." Instead you say, "This may be a little hard, but I can do it. I am glad I have a chance to do this. I am going to do my best. I know I can." You may think the MSP is a little hard, but you can do it. When you start the MSP, remember to think good thoughts. This will help you to be the best test hero you can be.

There was a girl named Gail,
Who thought she always would fail.
She said, "Tests are tough,
I'm not smart enough."
She had a sad end to her tale.

4. What Happens if I Don't Do Well on the Test?

The MSP is one way to find out how much you have learned by the third grade. It is important to try your best on the MSP, but remember, your friends, parents, and teachers will like you no matter how you do on this test.

There was a nice boy named Chad,
Who thought if he failed he was bad.
His teacher said, "That's not true.
I like you no matter how you do."
Now Chad is glad and not sad.

5. Don't Be Too Scared or Too Calm

Being too scared about tests will get in the way of doing your best. If you are scared, you won't be able to think clearly. If you are scared, your mind can't focus on the test. You think about other things. Your body might start to feel nervous. The chapter in this book called "Worry Less About Tests" will help you feel calmer about tests. Read that chapter so you can feel calmer about the MSP and other tests.

If you are too calm before taking a test, you might not do well. Sometimes, kids say, "I don't care about this!" They might not have pride in their school work. They may be nervous. They may think the MSP is "no big deal" and may try to forget about it. If you do not think a test is important and you try to forget about it, you are not thinking good thoughts. Don't be scared of the test, but don't forget about it. You can become a test hero and do your best if you take pride in your work.

There was a student named Claire,
Who usually said, "I don't care."
Her sister named Bess,
Always felt total stress.
They weren't a successful pair!

6. Don't Rush; Speeding Through the Test Doesn't Help

The last time you took a test, did you look around the room to see who finished first? If someone handed his or her paper in before you, did you feel like you needed to hurry up? Kids feel that way sometimes, but rushing through questions will not help you on the MSP. Finishing the MSP first, or second, or even third is not important. This may be a surprise to learn. Usually, we think speed is good. We hear about the fastest computer, the fastest runner, and the fastest car. Speed is exciting to think about, but working fast on the MSP will not make your test score better. Take your time, and you will be able to show what you know!

There was a third grader named Liz,
Who sped through her test like a whiz.
She thought she should race
At a very fast pace,
But it caused her to mess up her quiz.

7. Read Directions Carefully!

One of the best ways to become a test hero is to read directions. Directions help you understand what you're supposed to do. On the MSP, it is really important to take your time and to read directions. You may say, "Why should I read directions? I know what to do." Here's a story that may change your mind.

Imagine you are a famous baker. Everyone thinks you make the best cakes in Washington! One day, a group of kings and queens comes to Washington for an important visit. They ask you to bake a special cake for them. You have never baked this type of cake before. The kings and queens give you directions, but you don't read them. You think to yourself, "Who has time? I don't need directions. I know how to bake cakes." You don't read the directions but put them in a drawer. This is not a good idea. The directions tell you to bake the special cake at 250 degrees, but you bake the cake at 350 degrees! What do you get? A very crispy cake and very angry kings and queens. You should have read the directions!

Make sure you read directions slowly and repeat them to yourself. You should understand the directions before you begin the test.

There was a nice boy named Fred,
Who ignored almost all that he read.
The directions were easy,
But he said, "I don't need these!"
He should have read them instead.

8. Don't Get Stuck on One Question

Some of the questions on the MSP will be easy. Other questions might be a little harder. Don't let that worry you! If there is a question you're not sure how to answer, use your pencil to put a mark by the question. Remember, mark the question, not the answer choice bubbles. Once you have marked the hard question, move on to the next question. When you get to the end of the test, go back and try to answer the hard question. Once you have answered many easy questions, you might be able to answer the hard question with no problem.

If you circle a question and move on, you won't get stuck. This is a good hint. The MSP has lots of questions, so you will be able to show what you know. If there is a question that puzzles your mind, just go back to it later.

There was a sweet girl named Von,
Who got stuck and just couldn't go on.
She'd sit there and stare,
But the answer wasn't there.
Before she knew it, all the time was gone.

9. Use What You Know!

By the time you take the MSP, you will have been in school for four years. You went to kindergarten, first grade, and second grade, and now you are in the third grade. You were taught lots of things in school, but you learned many things in other places, too. You may have gathered information at the library, in a magazine, from TV, from your parents, and from lots of other places. Third graders have a lot of information in their brains!

Sometimes, third graders forget how much they know. You may see a question that your teacher has not talked about. This is OK. You may have heard about it somewhere else. Take a minute to think about all you know.

Let's say you were asked the following question.

> Melissa and her family go to Florida for a vacation. Melissa is excited about going to the beach and to an amusement park. She also really enjoys fresh orange juice. Melissa wants to walk to a store to buy an orange juice treat. The sign says the store is 200 yards away. If Melissa walks to the store, about how long will it take her?
>
> ○ A. About 5 minutes
> ○ B. About 30 minutes
> ○ C. About 1 hour

This seems like a hard question. You don't know how far 200 yards is. Stop and think for minute! You have heard the word "yard" before, but where? You may have heard it used in a football game; a football field is 100 yards. So 200 yards is about the length of two football fields. You know it will not take long to walk that far. Now you know the right answer; it will probably only take about 5 minutes. Even though you thought you didn't know the answer, you used the information you remembered from other places. You're on your way to becoming a test hero!

There was a boy named Drew,
Who forgot to use what he knew.
He had lots of knowledge.
He could have been in college,
But his correct answers were
very few.

10. Luck Isn't Enough!

Have you ever had a lucky number, a lucky color, or even a lucky hat? Everyone believes in luck. A famous football player always wears the same shoes game after game because he thinks they give him good luck. This doesn't make any sense. Wearing old, smelly shoes doesn't help him play well. But he believes in luck anyway. Believing in luck can be fun, but it is not going to help you do well on the MSP. The best way to do well is to PRACTICE! Listening to your teacher, practicing the hints you have learned in this book, and learning every day in the third grade will help you do your best.

There was a cool boy named Chuck,
Who thought taking tests was just luck.
He never prepared.
He said, "I'm not scared."
When his test scores appear, he should duck!

11. Recheck Your Answers

Everyone makes mistakes. Checking your work is very important. There once was a famous magician. He was very good at what he did, but he never checked his work. One night, he was getting ready for a big magic show. There were hundreds of people watching the show. The magician's wife said, "Check your pockets for everything you need." The magician didn't listen. "I've done this a million times," he said to himself. "I don't need to check my pockets." What a bad idea! When he got on stage, he reached his hand into an empty pocket—no magic tricks! Next time, he will recheck his pockets to do the best job possible! Going back and checking your work is very important. You can read a paragraph over again if there is something that you do not understand or something you forget. You will not be wasting time if you recheck your work. It is important to show what you know, not to show how fast you can go. Making sure you have put down the right answer is a good idea.

There was a quick girl named Jen,
Who read stuff once and never again.
It would have been nice
If she'd reread it twice.
Her scores would have been better then!

Helpful Hints from Other Third-Grade Test Heroes!

Third graders all over Washington have good ideas about tests. Here are some of them!

- Ask yourself, "Did I answer the question that was asked?" Carefully read the question so you can give the right answer.

- Read each answer choice before filling in an answer bubble. Sometimes, you read the first choice, and it seems right. But, when you get to the third choice, you realize that's the correct answer. If you had stopped with the first choice, you would have answered the question incorrectly. It is important to read all three choices before answering the question.

- Remember, the MSP is not trying to trick you. Do not look for trick answers. There will always be a right answer. If the answer choices do not look right, mark the question and go back to it later.

- Don't look around the room. Don't worry about how fast your friends are working, and don't worry about how well they are doing. Only worry about yourself. If you do that, you will do better on the test.

Reading

Introduction

The Reading Assessment of the Measurements of Student Progress (MSP) will measure how well you understand what you read. The Reading Assessment is based on the reading skills you have been taught in school through third grade. It is not meant to confuse or trick you but to allow you to have the best chance to show what you know.

The *Show What You Know® on the MSP for Grade 3, Student Workbook* includes a Reading Practice Tutorial that will help you practice your test-taking skills. Following the Reading Practice Tutorial, there are two full-length Reading Assessments. Both the Reading Practice Tutorial and the Reading Assessments have been created to model the Grade 3 Measurements of Student Progress for Reading.

About the Reading MSP

The Grade 3 Reading Assessment consists of six reading selections: two literary passages, two informational passages, and one paired passage, which could consist of informational/informational, informational/literary, or literary/literary. The Reading Assessment is given in one session.

For the Reading Assessment, you will read stories and other passages and answer some questions. There are two different types of questions. There are multiple-choice and short-answer questions. You may look back at the story or passage when you are answering the questions. However, you may not use resource materials during the Reading Assessment.

Item Distribution on the MSP for Grade 3 Reading

Text Types/ Strands	Number of Reading Selections	Number of Multiple Choice	Number of Short Answer
Literary	3	12	2–4
Comprehension		6	1–2
Analysis		6	1–2
Informational	3	12	2–4
Comprehension		6	1–2
Analysis		6	1–2
Total	6	24	6

Scoring

On the MSP for Grade 3 Reading Assessment, each multiple-choice item is worth one point. Short-answer items will be scored on a scale of zero to two points. Responses are scored with emphasis on communication of ideas. Conventions of writing (sentence structure, word choice, usage, grammar, and mechanics) are generally disregarded unless they substantially interfere with communications.

Typical Distribution of Score Points by Item Type*

Type	Number of Items	Total Possible Points
Multiple Choice	24	24
Short Answer	6	12
Total	30	36

2009 testing information.

Scoring Rules for Short-Answer Items

Scoring rules for items that assess <u>main ideas and details</u>:
A **2-point** response shows thorough comprehension of the main idea and important details. It uses ample, relevant information from text(s) to support responses.

A **1-point** response shows partial comprehension of the main idea and important details (may grasp main idea but show difficulty distinguishing between important and unimportant details; may miss part of fundamental who/what/where/when/why). It attempts to use information from text(s) to support responses; support may be limited or irrelevant.

A **0-point** response shows little or no understanding of the passage main ideas and details.

Scoring rules for items that assess <u>analysis, interpretation, and critical thinking about text</u>:
A **2-point** response analyzes appropriate information and/or makes thoughtful connections between whole texts/parts of texts. It develops thoughtful interpretations of text. It uses sufficient, relevant evidence from text(s) to support claims.

A **1-point** response analyzes limited information and/or makes superficial connections between whole texts/parts of texts. It develops conventional or simplistic interpretations of text. It attempts to use evidence from text(s) to support claims; support may be limited or irrelevant.

A **0-point** response shows little or no understanding of the passage main ideas and details.

Scoring rules for items that assess <u>summarizing and paraphrasing main ideas</u>:
A **2-point** response shows thorough comprehension of main ideas.

A **1-point** response shows partial comprehension of main ideas.

A **0-point** response shows little or no understanding of the passage main ideas and details.

Glossary

analogy: A comparison of two pairs that have the same relationship. The key is to discover the relationship between the first pair so you can choose the correct second pair (e.g., part-to-whole, opposites).

analysis: Separation of a whole into its parts for individual study.

analyze: To compare in order to rank items by importance or to provide reasons. Identify the important parts that make up the whole and determine how the parts are related to one another.

antonyms: Words that mean the opposite (e.g., *light* is an antonym of *dark*).

assumptions: Statements or thoughts taken to be true without proof.

audience: The people who read a written piece or hear the piece being read.

author's purpose: The reason an author writes, such as to entertain, to inform, or to persuade.

author's tone: The attitude the writer takes toward an audience, a subject, or a character. Tone is conveyed through the writer's choice of words and details. Examples of tone are happy, sad, angry, gentle, etc.

cause: The reason for an action, feeling, or response.

character: A person or an animal in a story, play, or other literary work.

compare: To use examples to show how things are alike.

context: The social or cultural situation in which the spoken or written word occurs. Often used to refer to the material surrounding an unknown word.

context clues: Information from the surrounding text that helps identify a word or word group. These could be words, phrases, sentences, illustrations, syntax, typographic signals, definitions, examples, and restatements.

contrast: To use examples to show how things are different.

details: Many small parts which help to tell a story.

draw conclusion: To make a decision or form an opinion after considering the facts from the text.

effect: A result of a cause.

fact: An actual happening or truth.

fiction: A selection that is made up rather than factually true. Examples of fiction are novels and short stories.

figurative language: Word images and figures of speech used to enrich language (e.g., simile, metaphor, personification).

flashback: An interruption in the present action of a story to flash backward and tell what happened at an earlier time. Flashbacks can occur anywhere in the story and usually give background information. An example of a flashback may be an adult flashing back to his childhood.

foreshadowing: A literary technique in which the author gives hints about an event before it happens.

generalize: To come to a broad idea or rule about something after considering particular facts.

genres: Categories of literary and informational works (e.g., biography, mystery, historical fiction, poetry).

graphic features: Features that illustrate information in text such as graphs, charts, maps, diagrams, tables, etc.

graphic organizer: Any illustration, chart, table, diagram, map, etc., used to help the reader interpret information about the text.

heading: A word or group of words at the top or front of a piece of writing.

idiom: A phrase or expression whose meaning cannot be understood using the ordinary meanings of the words in it (e.g., "You drive me crazy" or "Hold your horses.").

Glossary

infer: To make a guess based on facts and observations.

inference: An important idea or conclusion drawn from reasoning rather than directly stated in the text.

inform: To give knowledge; to tell.

informational/expository text: Text with the purpose of telling about details, facts, and information that are true (nonfiction). Sources for informational text include textbooks, encyclopedias, biographies, and newspaper articles.

irony: The use of words to convey the opposite of their literal meaning; the words say one thing but mean another.

literary devices: Techniques used to convey an author's message or voice (e.g. figurative language, similes, metaphors, etc.).

literary/narrative genres: Categories used to classify literary works, usually by form, technique, or content (e.g., novel, essay, short story, comedy, epic).

literary/narrative text: Text that describes actions or events, usually written as fiction. Examples are novels and short stories.

main idea: The main reason the passage was written—every passage has a main idea. Usually you can find the main idea in the topic sentence of each paragraph.

metaphor: A comparison between two unlike things in which one thing becomes another thing. An example of a metaphor is, "My bedroom is a junkyard!"

mood: The overall emotion created by the author.

nonfiction: A selection of writing that deals with real people, events, and places without changing any facts. Examples of nonfiction are an autobiography, a biography, an essay, a newspaper article, a magazine article, a personal diary, and a letter.

onomatopoeia: A term used to describe words whose pronunciations suggest their meaning (e.g., meow, buzz).

onset and rime: Parts of spoken language that are syllables. An onset is the initial consonant(s) sound of a syllable (the onset of bag is *b-*; of swim, *sw-*). A rime is the part of the syllable that contains the vowel and all that follows it (the rime of bag is *-ag*; of swim, *-im*). Not all syllables or words have an onset, but they all have a rime (e.g., the word or syllable "out" is a rime without an onset).

opinion: What one thinks about something or somebody; an opinion is not necessarily based on facts. Feelings and experiences usually help a person form an opinion.

organizational features: Tools the author uses to organize ideas (e.g., caption and headings).

passage: A selection or writing that may be fiction (literary/narrative) or nonfiction (informational/expository).

personification: A figure of speech in which a non-human thing or quality is talked about as if it were human (e.g., "The leaves danced along the driveway.").

persuade: To cause to do something by using reason or argument; to cause to believe something.

plot: A series of events that make up a story. Plot tells "what happens" in a story, novel, or narrative poem. The plot includes rising action (introduction of the characters and their problems), climax (the most exciting moment in the story), and resolution (the final part of the story when the characters' problems are solved and the story ends).

point of view: The position or angle from which the narrator tells the story. Stories can be told in first person: one of the characters is telling the story, using the personal pronoun "I." Another point of view is omniscient, or all-knowing: the narrator knows everything about the characters and their problems.

predict: The ability of the reader to know or expect that something is going to happen in a text before it does.

Glossary

prefix: A word part with its own meaning that is added to the beginning of a word to make a new word that has a different meaning. (e.g., *re–* is the prefix in the word **re**apply.)

primary source: The original source of resource information (e.g., newspaper, letter, encyclopedia, book).

prior knowledge: The knowledge that stems from previous experience. Note: prior knowledge is a key component of the schema theory of reading comprehension.

propaganda techniques: Methods used in creating propaganda, such as bandwagon, peer pressure, repetition, and testimonials/endorsements.

resource: A source of help or support.

root words: Meaningful base form of a complex word, after all affixes are removed. A root may be independent, or free, as "read" in unreadable, or may be dependent, or bound, as "-liter-" (from the Greek for letter) in illiterate.

sarcasm: A remark used to make fun of or put down someone or something. The remark is not sincere and is often actually intended to hurt someone's feelings.

schema: The accumulated knowledge that a person can draw from life experiences to help understand concepts, roles, emotions, and events.

secondary sources: Sources of information that are derived from primary, or original, sources.

sequential order: The arrangement or ordering of information, content, or ideas (e.g., a story told in chronological order describes what happened first, then second, then third, etc.).

setting: The time and place of a story or play. The setting helps to create the mood in a story, such as inside a spooky house or inside a shopping mall during the holidays.

simile: A comparison between two unlike things, using the words "like" or "as." "Her eyes are as big as saucers" is an example of a simile.

story elements: The important parts of the story, including characters, setting, plot, problem, and solution.

sub-genres: Genres within other genres (e.g., haiku is a sub-genre of poetry, and mystery is a sub-genre of fiction).

subplot: A minor collection of events in a novel or drama that have some connection with main plot and should, (1) comment on, (2) complicate/defeat, or (3) support the main plot.

suffix: A unit of meaning that is added to the end of a word to make a new word with a slightly different meaning. (e.g., *–ing* is the suffix in the word walk**ing**.)

summarize: To briefly retell a story by listing major idea(s).

supporting details: Statements that often follow the main idea. Supporting details give you more information about the main idea.

synonym: A word having a similar meaning to the meaning of another word (e.g., stone and rock).

text features: Prominent characteristics of a particular type of text, such as chapter titles, sub-headings, and bold-faced words in a history text.

text organizational structures: Expository text is structured in certain ways. The five text structures that students are most likely to encounter are cause/effect, compare/contrast, description, problem/solution, and chronological (or time) order.

theme: The major idea or topic that the author reveals in a literary work. A theme is usually not stated directly in the work. Instead, the reader has to think about all the details of the work and then make an inference (an educated guess) about what they all mean.

title: A name of a book, film, play, piece of music, or other work of art.

word families: A collection of words that share common orthographic rimes (e.g., thank, prank, dank).

Reading Tutorial

The Reading Practice Tutorial is made up of multiple-choice and short-answer questions. These questions show you how the skills you have learned in Reading class may be tested on the Reading MSP. The questions also give you a chance to practice your skills. If you have trouble with a question, talk with a parent or teacher.

Read each question carefully. If you do not know an answer, you may skip the question and come back to it later.

When you finish, check your answers.

Directions for the Reading Tutorial

Directions to the Student

Today you will take the Reading MSP Tutorial. This is to find out how well you understand what you read.

You will read stories and selections and answer some questions. You may look back at the story or selection when you are answering the questions. There are two different types of questions. There are multiple-choice questions that require you to choose the best answer. There are short-answer questions for which you will write phrases or sentences on the lines provided in your booklet.

Sample questions have been included. These sample questions do not relate to the selections you are about to read. They have been included to show you the different types of questions you will find in the booklet and how to mark or write your answers.

There are several important things to remember:
1. Read each selection. You may look back at the reading selection as often as you want.
2. The paragraphs in the reading passages are numbered. A question about a particular paragraph will refer to the paragraph number.
3. Read each question carefully. Then choose or write the answer that you think is best.
4. When you are supposed to write your answers, write them neatly and clearly on the lines provided. Cross out or erase any part of your work you do not want to include as part of your answer.
5. For short-answer questions, you may have more space than you need. You do not need to fill the whole space. Be sure to write complete answers.
6. When you are supposed to choose a multiple-choice answer, make sure you fill in the circle next to the answer.
7. Use only a **No. 2 pencil**, not a mechanical pencil or pen, to write or mark your answers directly in the space provided in your booklet. If you do not have a No. 2 pencil, ask your teacher to give you one.
8. The Reading MSP Assessment is un-timed, so be sure to take your time and give your best answer for each question. If you do not know the answer to a question, go to the next question. You can come back to that question later.
9. If you finish early, you may check over your work in this Reading section **only**.
10. When you reach the word **STOP** in your booklet, do not go on until you are told to turn the page.

Go on ▶

Sample Questions

To help you understand how to answer the test questions, look at the sample test questions below. These questions do not refer to the selections you are about to read. They are included to show you what the questions in the test are like and how to mark or write your answers.

Multiple-Choice Sample Question

For this type of question you will select the answer and fill in the circle next to it.

1 According to the story, which event happens first?

- ● A. Tony sees the skunk.
- ○ B. Tony drops his flashlight.
- ○ C. Tony's foot hurts.

For this sample question, the correct answer is A; therefore, the circle next to A is filled in.

Short-Answer Sample Question

For this type of question you will write a short answer consisting of a few phrases or sentences.

2 What are **two** similarities between Mrs. Sparrow and Mrs. Jay? Include information from the story in your answer.

Mrs. Sparrow and Mrs. Jay both go to the bird feeder every day at 6:00. Mrs. Jay says her husband built a wonderful nest for the family and Mrs. Sparrow says her husband also built a nest for the family.

Go on ▶

Directions: Read the story and answer the questions.

Red Riding Hood

1   When May was six years old, her grandma made her a red coat with a hood. She looked so pretty in it that the children all called her "Red Riding Hood."

2   One day her mama said, "I want you to take this cake and some butter to Grandma. Remember, go straight to grandma's house, do not stop on the way, and do not talk to strangers," her mama told her.

3   Red Riding Hood was very glad to go. She always had a good time at grandma's.

4   She put the things into her little basket and ran off.

5   When Red Riding Hood came to the woods, she met a big wolf.

6   "Where are you going?" asked the wolf.

7   Red Riding Hood said, "I am going to see my grandma. Mama has made her a cake and some butter."

8   "Does she live far?" asked the wolf.

9   "Yes," said Red Riding Hood, "in the white house by the mill."

10   "I will go too, and we shall see who will get there first," said the wolf.

11   The wolf ran off and took a short way, but Red Riding Hood stopped to pick some flowers.

12   When the wolf got to the house, he tapped on the door.

13   The grandma said, "Who is there?" The wolf made his voice as soft as he could. He said, "It is little Red Riding Hood, Grandma."

14   Then the old lady said, "Pull the string and the door will open."

15   The wolf pulled the string and the door opened.

Go on ▶

16   He ran in and swallowed the poor old lady.

17   Then he jumped into her bed and put on her cap.

18   When Red Riding Hood tapped on the door, the wolf called out, "Who is there?" Red Riding Hood said, "It is your little Red Riding Hood, Grandma."

19   Then the wolf said, "Pull the string and the door will open."

20   When she went in, she said, "Look, Grandma, see the cake and butter Mama has sent you."

21   "Thank you, dear, put them on the table and come here."

22   When Red Riding Hood went near the bed, she said, "Oh, Grandma, how big your arms are!"

23   "The better to hug you, my dear."

24   "How big your ears are, Grandma."

25   "The better to hear you, my dear."

26   "How big your eyes are, Grandma."

27   "The better to see you, my dear."

28   "How big your teeth are, Grandma!"

29   "The better to eat you."

30   Then the cruel wolf jumped up and swallowed poor little Red Riding Hood.

31   Just then a hunter came by. He heard Red Riding Hood scream. The hunter ran into the house and grabbed the old wolf by his feet.

32   When he turned the wolf upside down, out jumped Little Red Riding Hood and her grandma.

Go on ▶

Reading Tutorial   Show What You Know® on the MSP for Grade 3

1 What is the meaning of the word *tapped* as it is used in paragraph 12 of the story?

   ○ **A.** Danced

   ○ **B.** Knocked

   ○ **C.** Dug

2 Which sentence best states the main idea of the story?

   ○ **A.** Do not talk to strangers.

   ○ **B.** I am going to see my grandma.

   ○ **C.** The better to eat you.

3 What do you think Red Riding Hood will do the next time she meets the wolf? Support your prediction with information from the story.

_____

_____

_____

_____

_____

_____

_____

Go on ▶

4 Write a summary of the story. Include **three** main events from the story in your summary.

_____

_____

_____

_____

_____

_____

_____

Go on ▶

Directions: Read the story and answer the questions.

The Little Pine Tree

1   A little pine tree was in the woods.

2   It had no leaves. It had needles.

3   The little tree said, "I do not like needles. All the other trees in the woods have pretty leaves. I want leaves, too. But I will have better leaves. I want gold leaves."

4   Night came and the little tree went to sleep. A fairy came by and gave it gold leaves.

5   When the little tree woke it had leaves of gold.

6   It said, "Oh, I am so pretty! No other tree has gold leaves."

7   Night came.

8   A man came by with a bag. He saw the gold leaves. He took them all and put them into his bag.

9   The poor little tree cried, "I do not want gold leaves again. I will have glass leaves."

10   So the little tree went to sleep. The fairy came by and put the glass leaves on it.

11   The little tree woke and saw its glass leaves.

12   How pretty they looked in the sunshine! No other tree was so bright.

13   Then a wind came up. It blew and blew.

14   The glass leaves all fell from the tree and were broken.

Go on ▶

15   Again the little tree had no leaves. It was very sad and said, "I will not have gold leaves, and I will not have glass leaves. I want green leaves. I want to be like the other trees."

16   And the little tree went to sleep. When it woke, it was like other trees. It had green leaves.

17   A goat came by. He saw the green leaves on the little tree. The goat was hungry and he ate all the leaves.

18   Then the little tree said, "I do not want any leaves. I will not have green leaves, nor glass leaves, nor gold leaves. I like my needles best."

19   And the little tree went to sleep. The fairy gave it what it wanted.

20   When it woke, it had its needles again. Then the little pine tree was happy.

Go on ▶

Reading Tutorial

5 According to the story, which event happens first?

◯ **A.** The little tree asks for gold leaves.

◯ **B.** The glass leaves fall from the tree.

◯ **C.** The goat eats all the leaves.

6 Based on the story, how does the little pine tree feel about the other trees in the woods?

◯ **A.** The little pine tree is mad at the other trees.

◯ **B.** The little pine tree is jealous of the other trees.

◯ **C.** The little pine tree is happy for the other trees.

Go on ▶

Show What You Know® on the MSP for Grade 3 Reading Tutorial

7 What problem does the little pine tree face?

_____

_____

What is **one** step the little pine tree takes to solve this problem? Include information from the story in your answer.

_____

_____

_____

_____

_____

8 According to the story, what happened when the wind blew and blew?

○ **A.** A man came by and put the gold leaves in his bag.

○ **B.** A goat ate all the leaves.

○ **C.** The glass leaves fell from the tree and were broken.

Go on ▶

Directions: Read the selection and answer the questions.

A Sign of Pride

1   An important sign of the United States is our flag. Our flag stands for the land. It stands for the people. It stands for the government.

2   On June 14, 1777, the Continental Congress decided on a flag for the United States that would have 13 stripes. The stripes would be red and white. The first stripe would be red. The next stripe would be white. The stripe after that would be red, and so on. The Continental Congress also said the flag would have a group of 13 white stars on a blue background. The 13 stripes stood for the first 13 colonies. These 13 colonies were the first states in the United States. The 13 stars stood for the number of states in the United States at that time.

3   The Continental Congress did not say how the stars should be arranged. On some flags, 12 stars were placed in a circle with one star in the middle. On others, the 13 stars were placed in a circle.

4   As new states became part of the United States, more stars and stripes were added to the flag. People soon thought the flag had too many stripes. The Flag Act of 1818 stated that the American flag would only have 13 stripes, one stripe for each of the first 13 colonies. The Flag Act also said the American flag should have one white star for each state in the United States. In 1846, the flag had 28 stars. By 1861, the number of stars was 34. In 1898, the flag had 45 stars. The last change to the flag was in 1960. A star was added for the state of Hawaii. The flag with 50 stars is the one we use today.

5   The American flag has had several nicknames. Our country's earliest flag was known as the Continental flag, or the Congress colors. Today, it is called the Stars and Stripes. It is also called Old Glory or the Red, White, and Blue. No matter what name is used, the flag we see flying today is an important sign of pride for our country.

Go on ▶

9 Who would find the information in the selection most useful?

○ A. A student writing a report on flags

○ B. A student writing a report on Hawaii

○ C. A student writing a report on stars

10 What is most likely the author's purpose for writing the selection?

○ A. To entertain readers with a story about the U.S. flag

○ B. To inform readers about the history of the U.S. flag

○ C. To demonstrate to readers how to create their own flag

Go on ▶

The Harrison Elementary Press
A Newspaper Written By Kids, For Kids

March Issue Science Section, Page 1

FROGS AND TOADS
By Federico Garcia

1   It's important to look to see if the animal you are about to kiss is a frog or a toad. You may never find a handsome prince if you kiss the wrong amphibian. Can you tell the difference between a frog and a toad?

2   It is easy to confuse frogs and toads just by looking at them. They are both amphibians. This means they can live both in water and on land. They both are coldblooded. This means their body temperatures are the same as the air temperatures around them. They have to look for cool, shady places to rest if they become too hot. Frogs and toads look for warm, sunny places if they are too cold. Both animals are vertebrates. This means they have spines. Their body shape is almost the same. Their eyes stick out from their faces, so they can see in most directions without turning their heads.

3   Frogs and toads use their long, sticky tongues to catch insects to eat. Both frogs and toads swallow their food whole.

4   How are frogs and toads different? Frogs are better swimmers and jumpers because they have long back legs. A toad's back legs are shorter. Frogs are more likely to be found near water. Toads often live in drier places. Most frogs have four webbed feet. Toads do not have webs on their back feet. The skin of a frog is smooth and damp. Toads have drier skin that is covered with bumps called glands. Frogs have teeth in their upper jaws and no teeth in their lower jaws. Toads have no teeth at all.

5   As you can see, frogs and toads are not the same type of amphibian. Of course, a frog turning into a handsome prince only happens in fairy tales. Who would kiss a frog or a toad anyway?

Go on ▶

11 Which sentence from the selection is an opinion?

- ○ **A.** Frogs and toads are coldblooded.
- ○ **B.** Frogs and toads swallow their food whole.
- ○ **C.** It is easy to confuse frogs and toads just by looking at them.

12 The author's purpose for writing this selection may have been to inform the reader about frogs and toads. Support this purpose with **two** details from the selection.

_____

_____

_____

_____

_____

_____

Go on ▶

13 How might the selection be useful to someone who wants to get a frog for a pet? Include **two** details from the selection in your answer.

_____

_____

_____

_____

_____

_____

_____

_____

STOP

Reading Assessment One

Introduction

Reading Assessment One is made up of multiple-choice and short-answer questions. These questions show you how the skills you have learned in Reading class may be tested on the Reading MSP. The questions also give you a chance to practice your skills. If you have trouble with a question, talk with a parent or teacher.

Read each question carefully. If you do not know an answer, you may skip the question and come back to it later.

When you finish, check your answers.

Directions for Reading Assessment One

Directions to the Student

Today you will take the Reading MSP Assessment One. This is to find out how well you understand what you read.

You will read stories and selections and answer some questions. You may look back at the story or selection when you are answering the questions. There are two different types of questions. There are multiple-choice questions that require you to choose the best answer. There are short-answer questions for which you will write phrases or sentences on the lines provided in your booklet.

Sample questions have been included. These sample questions do not relate to the selections you are about to read. They have been included to show you the different types of questions you will find in the booklet and how to mark or write your answers.

There are several important things to remember:
1. Read each selection. You may look back at the reading selection as often as you want.
2. The paragraphs in the reading passages are numbered. A question about a particular paragraph will refer to the paragraph number.
3. Read each question carefully. Then choose or write the answer that you think is best.
4. When you are supposed to write your answers, write them neatly and clearly on the lines provided. Cross out or erase any part of your work you do not want to include as part of your answer.
5. For short-answer questions, you may have more space than you need. You do not need to fill the whole space. Be sure to write complete answers.
6. When you are supposed to choose a multiple-choice answer, make sure you fill in the circle next to the answer.
7. Use only a **No. 2 pencil**, not a mechanical pencil or pen, to write or mark your answers directly in the space provided in your booklet. If you do not have a No. 2 pencil, ask your teacher to give you one.
8. The Reading MSP Assessment is un-timed, so be sure to take your time and give your best answer for each question. If you do not know the answer to a question, go to the next question. You can come back to that question later.
9. If you finish early, you may check over your work in this Reading section **only**.
10. When you reach the word **STOP** in your booklet, do not go on until you are told to turn the page.

Go on ▶

Direction: Read the story and answer the questions.

The Farmer and His Three Sons

1   A farmer who had worked hard all his life was taken sick. He knew that he must soon die. He called his three sons about his bed to give them some advice.

2   "My sons," said he, "keep all of the land which I leave you. Do not sell any of it, for there is a treasure in the soil. I shall not tell you where to hunt for it, but if you try hard to find it, and do not give up, you will surely succeed.

3   "As soon as the harvest[1] is over, begin your search with plow, and spade, and rake. Turn every foot of earth, then turn it again and again. The treasure is there."

4   After the father died, the sons gathered in the harvest. As soon as the grain had been cared for, they planned to search for the hidden treasure. The farm was divided into three equal parts. Each son agreed to dig carefully his part.

5   Every foot of soil was turned by the plow or by the spade[2]. It was next harrowed[3] and raked, but no treasure was found. That seemed very strange.

6   "Father was an honest man and a wise man," said the youngest son. "He would never have told us to hunt for the treasure if it were not here. Do you not remember that he said, 'Turn the soil again and again'? He surely thought the treasure worth hunting for."

7   "Our land is in such good condition now that we might as well sow winter wheat," said the oldest son. His brothers agreed to this and the wheat was sown.

8   The next harvest was so great that it surprised them. No neighbor's field bore[4] so many bushels[5] of wheat to the acre. The sons were pleased with their success.

---

[1] *harvest: the gathering in of a crop*
[2] *spade: a tool used for digging*
[3] *harrow(ed): to break up and level plowed ground*
[4] *bore: produced*
[5] *bushel: a unit of dry measure for grain*

Go on ▶

9   After the wheat was harvested, they met to make plans for searching again for the hidden treasure. The second son said:

10   "I have been thinking ever since our big harvest that perhaps father knew how this search would turn out. We have much gold. We did not find it in a hole in the ground, but we found it by digging. If we had not cultivated[6] our fields well, we should not have had such a crop of wheat. Our father was wise; we have dug for the treasure and have found it.

11   "We will cultivate the ground still better next year and make the soil rich; then we shall find more treasure."

12   The other sons agreed to this. "It is good to work for what we get," they said.

13   Year after year the farm was well tilled and bore good crops. The sons became rich, and they had two things much better than wealth—good health and happiness.

---

[6] cultivated: to have prepared soil or land for growing crops

Go on ▶

1 According to the story, which event happens last?

- ○ A. The sons are pleased with their success.
- ○ B. The father tells the sons there is treasure in the soil.
- ○ C. The sons agree it is good to work for what they get.

2 According to the story, where does the story take place?

- ○ A. In a city
- ○ B. On a farm
- ○ C. In a town

3 According to the story, which sentence explains why winter wheat was planted?

- ○ A. "Every foot of soil was turned by the plow or by the spade."
- ○ B. "The next harvest was so great that it surprised them."
- ○ C. "Year after year the farm was well tilled and bore good crops."

Go on ▶

4 Any of these titles could be another title for the story. Choose the title you think best fits the story.

Buried Treasure

The Big Harvest

Rich Soil

Support your choice with **two** details from the story.

_____
_____
_____
_____
_____
_____
_____
_____

5 What does the father mean when he says, "Do not sell any of it, for there is a treasure in the soil" in paragraph 2 of the story?

○ **A.** The treasure buried in the soil will make the sons rich.

○ **B.** The soil is the treasure that will make the sons rich.

○ **C.** The harvest the soil will provide is the treasure that will make the sons rich.

Go on ▶

Directions: Read the selection and answer the questions.

Clouds

1   Clouds are little drops of water or ice that float together through the air. Clouds come in different shapes and sizes.

2   There are three different kinds of clouds. You can tell the kind of cloud by the way the cloud looks and where it is in the sky. Some clouds are low in the sky, some are in the middle, and some are high in the sky.

3   The highest clouds in the sky are cirrus clouds. Some people think cirrus clouds look like thin white feathers. Others call cirrus clouds "mares' tails" because they look like the long tails of horses. Because cirrus clouds are so high in the sky where the temperature is very cold, cirrus clouds are made of tiny ice crystals. Cirrus clouds move quickly across the sky at about 200 miles an hour.

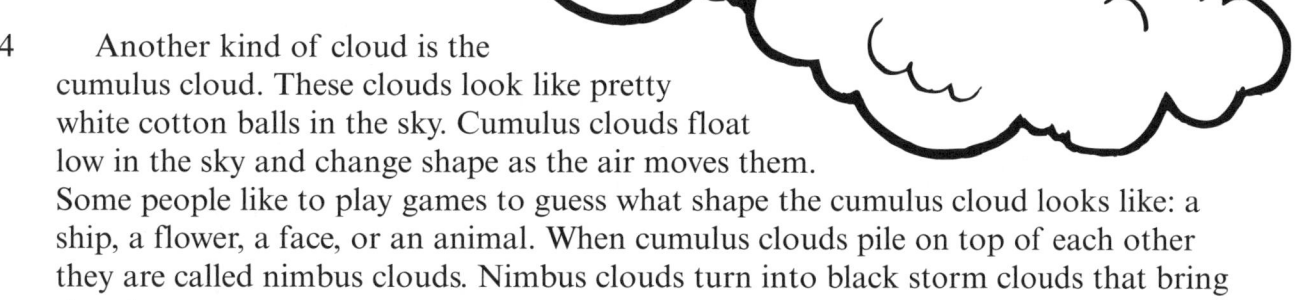

4   Another kind of cloud is the cumulus cloud. These clouds look like pretty white cotton balls in the sky. Cumulus clouds float low in the sky and change shape as the air moves them. Some people like to play games to guess what shape the cumulus cloud looks like: a ship, a flower, a face, or an animal. When cumulus clouds pile on top of each other they are called nimbus clouds. Nimbus clouds turn into black storm clouds that bring thunderstorms.

5   Stratus clouds are low in the sky. They look like long, gray blanket clouds. Rain and snow may fall from stratus clouds. Stratus clouds often hide the sun and the moon.

Go on ▶

6 Who would find the information in the selection most useful?

○ **A.** A student writing a report on clouds

○ **B.** A student writing a report on weather

○ **C.** A student writing a report on temperature

7 What is the meaning of the word *float* in paragraph 4 of the selection?

○ **A.** To go from job to job

○ **B.** To flood or irrigate land

○ **C.** To move slowly and lightly through the air

Go on ▶

8 Any of these headings could be used for the paragraph 4. Choose the heading that best fits the paragraph.

Cotton Balls in the Sky

Cloud Watching

Cumulus Clouds

Support your choice with **two** details from the selection.

_____

_____

_____

_____

_____

_____

_____

Go on ▶

9 What is most likely the author's purpose for writing the selection?

○ A. To entertain the reader with a story about clouds

○ B. To inform the reader about different types of clouds

○ C. To demonstrate how clouds create thunderstorms

10 Which sentence from the selection is an opinion?

○ A. "Stratus clouds are low in the sky."

○ B. "These clouds look like pretty white cotton balls in the sky."

○ C. "Cumulus clouds float low in the sky and change shape as the air moves them."

Go on ▶

Directions: Read the poem and answer the questions.

The Raindrops' New Dresses

"We're so tired of these gray dresses!"
Cried the little drops of rain,
As they came down helter-skelter[1]
From the Nimbus cloud fast train.

5   And they bobbed against each other
In a spiteful[2] sort of way,
Just like children when bad temper
Gets the upper hand some day.

    Then the Sun peeped out a minute.
10 "Dears, be good and do not fight,
I have ordered you new dresses,
Dainty robes of purest white."

Ah! then all the tiny raindrops
Hummed a merry glad refrain[3],
15 And the old folks cried:
"How pleasant
Is the music of the rain!"

Just at even, when the children
Had been safely tucked in bed,
20 There was such a rush and bustle
In the dark clouds overhead!

Then those raindrops hurried earthward,
At the North Wind's call, you know,
And the wee folks, in the morning,
25 Laughed to see the flakes of snow.

---

[1] *helter-skelter: with hurry and confusion*
[2] *spiteful: having or showing a desire to cause harm or pain to others*
[3] *refrain: a melody or tune*

Go on ▶

11 According to the poem, which event happens last?

- A. The children went to sleep.
- B. The Sun peeped out.
- C. It was raining.

12 Which sentence best summarizes the poem?

- A. When it is cold enough, rain turns into snow.
- B. It snows when the children go to sleep.
- C. Adults like to listen to the sound of the rain.

Go on ▶

13 Based on the poem, describe how the raindrops feel about their gray dresses.

_____

_____

Support your answer with **one** detail from the poem.

_____

_____

_____

_____

_____

Go on ▶

Reading Assessment One Show What You Know® on the MSP for Grade 3

14 Which word could the author have use in paragraph 6 instead of *hurried*?

○ **A.** Rushed

○ **B.** Strolled

○ **C.** Tripped

15 The author of Clouds states, "Nimbus clouds turn into black storm clouds that bring thunderstorms." Include **two** examples from The Raindrops' New Dresses that demonstrate how nimbus clouds bring thunderstorms.

_____

_____

_____

_____

_____

_____

_____

Go on ▶

Directions: Read the selection and answer the questions.

A Journey Through Washington

1. The Lewis and Clark Expedition[1] was one of the greatest explorations in American History. President Thomas Jefferson hired Lewis and Clark to map the way west through the new Louisiana Territory[2] to the Pacific Ocean.

2. The Expedition left its winter camp near St. Louis on May 14, 1804 and went up the Missouri River. In October, they reached the Mandan villages in what is now North Dakota. This is where they spent the winter. They headed west in the spring of 1805.

3. On October 10, 1805, they came to what is now the state of Washington. As they traveled down the Snake and Columbia Rivers, the explorers began to see signs that they were nearing the Pacific Coast.

4. On November 15, 1805, the Expedition reached "Station Camp," the place they called the "End of Our Voyage." From this camp, they took side trips along the river's north bank to Cape Disappointment. On November 24, the party decided to explore the south side of the river and set up winter camp at Fort Clatsop (near what is now Astoria, Oregon).

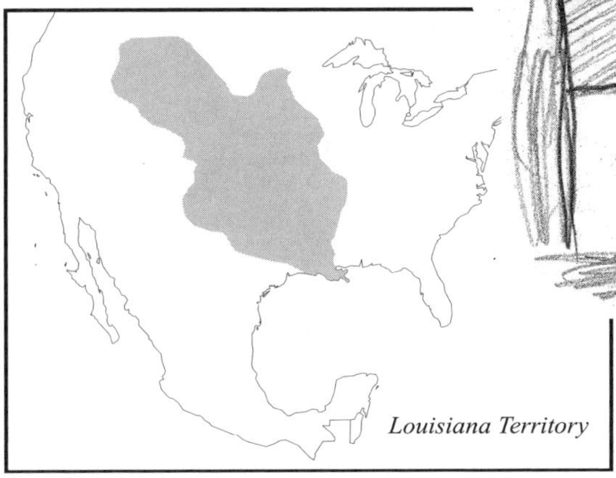

Louisiana Territory

---

[1] *Expedition: a trip made by a group of people to explore unknown territory*
[2] *Louisiana Territory: land bought by the U.S. from France in 1803; it extended from the Mississippi River to the Rocky Mountains and from the Gulf of Mexico to Canada*

5   As soon as they thought the mountains would be passable[3] in the spring, Lewis and Clark and their party left Fort Clatsop. Following the river—first in canoes and then on land—they retraced[4] their route up the Columbia to the mouth of the Walla Walla River. Here, American Indians told them of a path to the Snake River. By following this shortcut, they saved many miles on their return journey. The route from the Columbia River to the Snake River was one of the longest by land of their trip.

6   On May 5, 1806, the Expedition left what is now the state of Washington and headed east, reaching St. Louis on September 23, 1806.

7   The Lewis and Clark Expedition completed an amazing mission. The party made many important discoveries about the native peoples of the region, the geography, wildlife, and plants of the American West.

---

[3] passable: capable of being crossed or traveled on
[4] retraced: went back over a path or route again

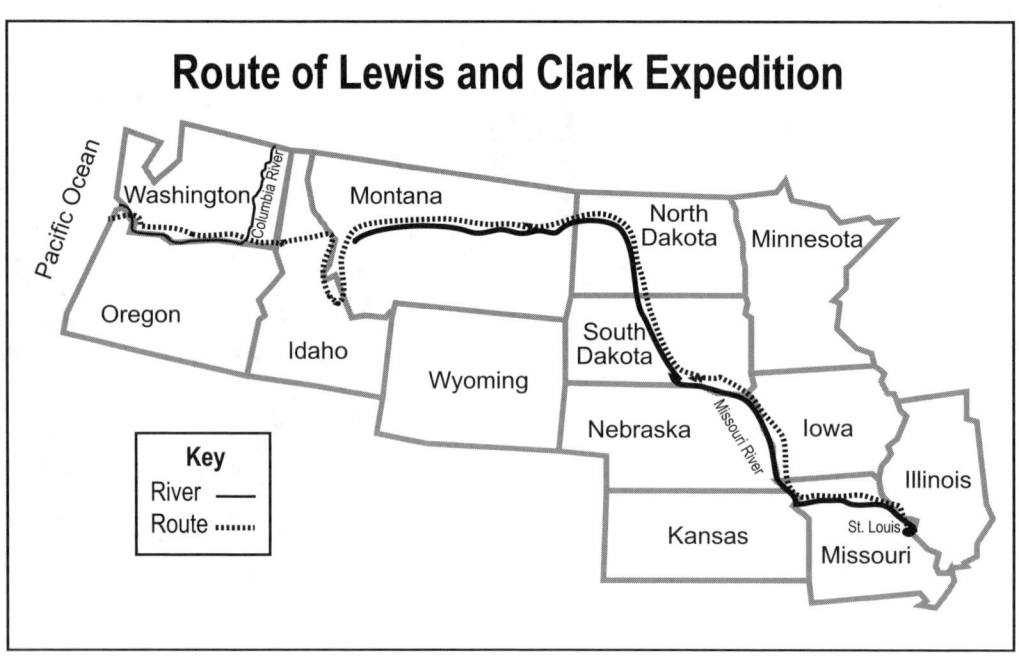

Go on ▶

16 What is the meaning of the word *route* in paragraph 5 of the selection?

○ A. A path or road for traveling from one place to another

○ B. To uncover something, especially after a search

○ C. To search for something by poking around or digging

17 According to the selection, what happens when the mountains became passable in the spring?

○ A. The Expedition set up winter camp.

○ B. The Expedition left Fort Clatsop.

○ C. The Expedition reached the Mandan villages.

18 Which sentence is the best summary of paragraph 2?

○ A. The Expedition followed a short path from the Columbia River to the Snake River.

○ B. The Expedition spent the winter in a village in what is now North Dakota before heading west.

○ C. In October of 1805, the Expedition traveled down river to arrive near the Pacific coast.

Go on ▶

19 Who would find the information in the selection most useful?

- ○ **A.** A family planning a trip to Washington State
- ○ **B.** An author writing a story about rafting on the Columbia River
- ○ **C.** A teacher presenting a lesson on American history of the 1800s

20 What is most likely the author's purpose for writing this selection?

- ○ **A.** To persuade the reader to go on an expedition like Lewis and Clark
- ○ **B.** To inform the reader about the history of the Lewis and Clark Expedition
- ○ **C.** To demonstrate an expedition in 1805 to the reader

Go on ▶

Directions: Read the story and answer the questions.

The Key
by Andrea Karch Balas

1   Emma noticed a small, white box on the stairs. She picked it up carefully and opened it to find a small key wrapped in a lace handkerchief. Faded pink and blue flowers decorated the delicate handkerchief, and the initials "A.B." were stitched into one corner. Emma thought that it could belong to her grandmother because her name, Abby Brown, matched the initials.

2   As Emma examined the key, she saw that it was a dull, golden color. It was about as long as her index finger and seemed heavy for its size. There was a bit of crumpled blue ribbon looped through the hole at the top of the key. Emma thought to herself that the key must be very old because it was so worn. Emma wanted to find her grandmother and ask her about the key. As she went from room to room looking for her grandmother, Emma imagined that there might be wonderful treasures somewhere for that key to unlock. Then, Emma remembered that Gramma had gone to the store. Emma's questions would have to wait until she returned.

3   Emma was sitting on the porch step when Gramma returned. She slowly removed the key from her pocket and held it up for Gramma to see. "Look what I found—is it yours?" Emma asked. A broad smile appeared on Gramma's face as she inspected the key. "I thought I had lost this," Gramma said. "This key opens a very special box I have stored in the attic." Then, Gramma took Emma's hand and said, "Come with me. I have something to show you."

4   Emma and her grandmother walked through the house to the back stairs that led up to the attic. As they climbed the steep steps to the storage place, Emma's mind raced with thoughts about that special box. She wondered what it would look like and, most importantly, what would be inside the box.

Go on ▶

21 Which word best describes how Gramma felt about Emma?

- **A.** Angry
- **B.** Upset
- **C.** Kind

22 Any of these phrases could identify the author's purpose for writing the story. Choose the phrase that best describes the author's purpose for writing the story.

To entertain

To describe

To inform

Support your choice with **two** details from the story.

_____
_____
_____
_____
_____
_____
_____
_____

Go on ▶

23 According to the story, after Emma went from room to room looking for her grandmother, what did she do next?

- A. Emma waited on the porch step for Gramma to return.
- B. Emma examined the key.
- C. Emma wondered what would be inside the box.

24 Which sentence best summarizes the story?

- A. "Emma noticed a small, white box on the stairs."
- B. "There was a bit of crumpled blue ribbon looped through the hole at the top of the key."
- C. "This key opens a very special box I have stored in the attic."

25 What is the meaning of the word *examined* as it is used in paragraph 2 of the story?

- A. To inspect a patient in order to determine his or her condition or health
- B. To ask questions of a witness or other party to a case in a court of law
- C. To inspect or study somebody or something in detail

Go on ▶

Directions: Read the story and answer the questions.

Max, the Mischievous Macaw
by Judy Cafmeyer

1   Billy knew the routine well. It happened almost every day. It was Billy's job to look for Max. Where would he find Max? What mischief had Max gotten into? Did Max destroy anything in the house? These were the questions Billy asked himself as he searched all the rooms looking for Max.

2   Macaws are well-known for enjoying puzzles, and perhaps Max saw picking the latch on his cage as a fun puzzle to solve. At first, it was easy to find Max because the macaw wasn't familiar with the new surroundings. The bird would stay near the cage, which stood in the corner of the dining room next to the kitchen. Billy usually found Max sitting on the kitchen counter with the remnants of a pretzel feast scattered around. Recently, however, Max had started exploring other areas of the house.

3   It was Max's curiosity that caused Billy's daily task to begin. He had to locate Max and hope the cleanup would be easy.

Go on ▶

26 Any of these words could describe Max in the story. Choose the word you think best describes Max.

Naughty   Playful   Difficult

Support your choice with **two** details from the story.

_____
_____
_____
_____
_____
_____
_____
_____

27 According to the story, after Max got out of his cage, what did he do next?

○ **A.** Eat pretzels

○ **B.** Finish a puzzle

○ **C.** Pick the latch on the cage

Go on ▶

28 Based on the information in the story, what do you predict Billy will do with Max?

○ **A.** Billy will let Max out of his cage.

○ **B.** Billy will put Max back in his cage.

○ **C.** Billy will put Max in the kitchen.

29 What is the main idea of the story?

○ **A.** Max likes pretzels.

○ **B.** Max likes puzzles.

○ **C.** Max is curious.

30 What is the meaning of the word *remnants* as it is used in paragraph 2 of the story?

○ **A.** Covers

○ **B.** Crumbs

○ **C.** Chunks

STOP

Reading Assessment Two

Introduction

Reading Assessment Two is made up of multiple-choice and short-answer questions. These questions show you how the skills you have learned in Reading class may be tested on the Reading MSP. The questions also give you a chance to practice your skills. If you have trouble with a question, talk with a parent or teacher.

Read each question carefully. If you do not know an answer, you may skip the question and come back to it later.

When you finish, check your answers.

Reading Assessment Two

Directions for Reading Assessment Two

Directions to the Student

Today you will take the Reading MSP Assessment Two. This is to find out how well you understand what you read.

You will read stories and selections and answer some questions. You may look back at the story or selection when you are answering the questions. There are two different types of questions. There are multiple-choice questions that require you to choose the best answer. There are short-answer questions for which you will write phrases or sentences on the lines provided in your booklet.

Sample questions have been included. These sample questions do not relate to the selections you are about to read. They have been included to show you the different types of questions you will find in the booklet and how to mark or write your answers.

There are several important things to remember:
1. Read each selection. You may look back at the reading selection as often as you want.
2. The paragraphs in the reading passages are numbered. A question about a particular paragraph will refer to the paragraph number.
3. Read each question carefully. Then choose or write the answer that you think is best.
4. When you are supposed to write your answers, write them neatly and clearly on the lines provided. Cross out or erase any part of your work you do not want to include as part of your answer.
5. For short-answer questions, you may have more space than you need. You do not need to fill the whole space. Be sure to write complete answers.
6. When you are supposed to choose a multiple-choice answer, make sure you fill in the circle next to the answer.
7. Use only a **No. 2 pencil**, not a mechanical pencil or pen, to write or mark your answers directly in the space provided in your booklet. If you do not have a No. 2 pencil, ask your teacher to give you one.
8. The Reading MSP Assessment is un-timed, so be sure to take your time and give your best answer for each question. If you do not know the answer to a question, go to the next question. You can come back to that question later.
9. If you finish early, you may check over your work in this Reading section **only**.
10. When you reach the word **STOP** in your booklet, do not go on until you are told to turn the page.

Directions: Read the story and answer the questions.

Seren and the Ladybug

1. It was 9:00 a.m. on the last day of school. Seren had a big smile on her face. She walked up to the front door. She reached for the handle and stopped. Sitting on the door handle was a small red bug with black spots. It was the prettiest bug Seren had seen. She held up her hand to the door. The bug crawled onto her finger.

2. Seren opened the door. She walked to her third-grade classroom for the last time.

3. Seren's friends were so happy about the last-day-of-school party. They could hardly sit still. They all yelled, "Hi!" and waved at Seren when she came into the room. Seren waved back with her free hand. She set her bag down on her chair and walked up to Ms. Rolson's desk.

4. "Good morning, Seren," Ms. Rolson said with a smile. She saw the small red bug on Seren's hand. "That's a very pretty ladybug you have."

5. "Ms. Rolson," Seren asked, "Is this really a bug? It looks like a bug. But it's so much prettier than all the other bugs I have seen. It's hard to believe that it's the same."

6. Ms. Rolson reached out her hand to Seren's. The ladybug crawled to the teacher's hand. "Yes, Seren, it is a bug. A ladybug is a type of beetle." Ms. Rolson held up her hand so that Seren could see the bug more closely. "See these hard, shiny parts with the spots on them?" Seren nodded. "All beetles have these. They're a type of wings. Instead of being used for flying, they're used to protect what's under them."

7. "What's under them that would need to be protected?" Seren was becoming more curious about her bug.

8. "Most of the time, it's another set of wings. Many types of beetles can fly, but not as well as other kinds of bugs, such as flies. They also protect the beetles' mid-sections." At that moment, the ladybug opened its outer wings. It flew away with the softer wings hidden below. Seren jumped backward in surprise. Then, she began to laugh.

9. "Wow, Ms. Rolson. I never thought I would learn so much on the last day of school!"

Go on ▶

1 What is the main idea of the story?

  ○ **A.** Seren was excited about ending school for the year.

  ○ **B.** Seren learned about a creature she found on her last day of school.

  ○ **C.** Seren was working on a report about ladybugs on her last day of school.

2 According to the story, which event happens first?

  ○ **A.** Seren saw a ladybug on a door handle.

  ○ **B.** A ladybug crawled onto Seren's finger.

  ○ **C.** A ladybug flew away from Seren.

Go on ▶

3 Any of these words could describe Seren in the story. Choose the word you think best describes Seren.

Curious   Caring   Friendly

Support your answer with **two** details from the story.

_____

_____

_____

_____

_____

_____

_____

_____

Go on ▶

4 Which sentence explains why ladybugs have hard wings?

- A. "A ladybug is a type of beetle."
- B. "Instead of being used for flying, they're used to protect what's under them."
- C. "Many types of beetles can fly, but not as well as other kinds of bugs, such as flies."

5 What is most likely the author's purpose for writing the story?

- A. To persuade the reader to search for beetles
- B. To demonstrate to the reader what happens on the last day of school
- C. To inform the reader about the characteristics of ladybugs

Go on ▶

Directions: Read the selection and answer the questions.

The Hidden Message

1	Secret messages aren't just for detectives and spies. Some of them, the kinds that use words in place of other words or put letters in a different order, can be very hard. These are the types of secret messages that kings and rulers used when messages had to be carried on foot or by horse. If an enemy caught a soldier carrying one of these secret messages, the person sending the message hoped that the enemy would not be able to read it.

2	Because the messages sent out by kings and rulers were usually very important, the people who were writing the secret codes wanted to make them hard to read. Not all secret codes have to be so hard, though. There are some ways that you can make simple secret messages to send to your friends.

3	One way you can send secret messages is to use invisible ink. Invisible ink can be made in a few different ways. One way is to use lemon juice to write on a piece of paper. You can write by dipping a toothpick or the tip of a dried-out pen into the lemon juice, then use it to write as you would normally. Let the juice dry completely and give the secret message to a friend. The friend will need a parent or another adult to help read the message. Have the parent or adult hold the message up close to a light bulb, or have them hold a hot iron an inch or two above the paper. When the paper gets hot, the lemon juice will darken and the message will appear.

4	There is another way to write an invisible message using only art supplies. Write on a piece of white paper with a white crayon. It may be difficult to see what you are writing, but when you're done, it will look like nothing is there. Anyone who wants to read the message can use water-based paint to paint over the side with the writing on it. The secret message will appear.

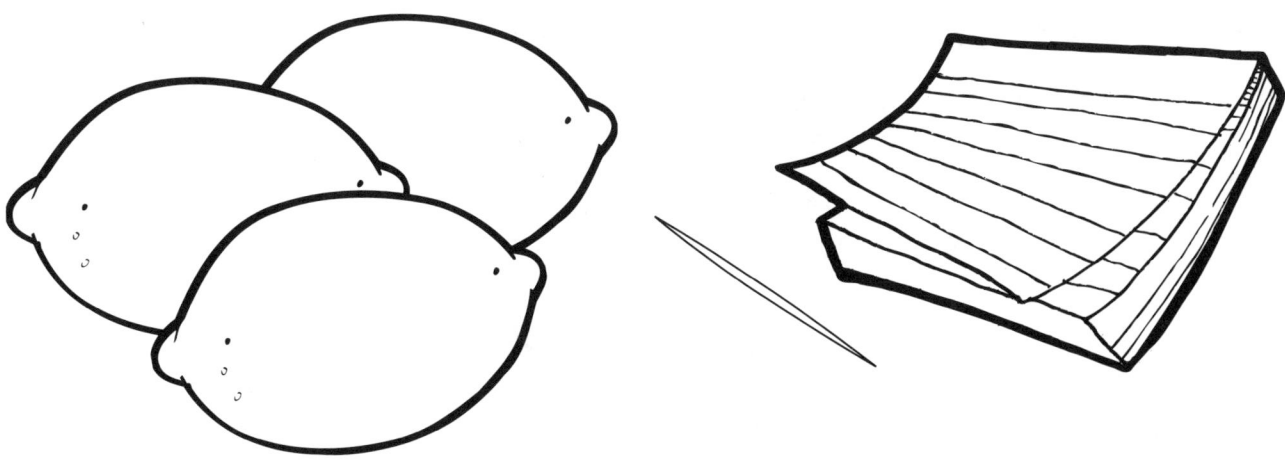

Go on ▶

6 What is the meaning of the word *invisible* in paragraph 3 of the selection?

- ○ A. Cannot be seen
- ○ B. Able to be seen
- ○ C. Not in the sea

7 Which sentence explains why secret messages were used by kings and rulers?

- ○ A. "Secret messages aren't just for detectives and spies."
- ○ B. "If an enemy caught a soldier carrying one of these secret messages, the person sending the message hoped that the enemy would not be able to read it."
- ○ C. "Anyone who wants to read the message can use water-based paint to paint over the side with the writing on it."

8 According to the selection, what happens when paper with lemon juice on it is heated?

- ○ A. The lemon juice will disappear.
- ○ B. The lemon juice will create a hole in the paper.
- ○ C. The lemon juice will darken.

Go on ▶

9 According to the selection, which idea does the author of the selection discuss last?

- ○ A. One way to send secret messages is to use invisible ink.
- ○ B. One way to send secret messages is to use art supplies.
- ○ C. One way to send secret messages is to put words in a different order.

10 How might the selection be useful to someone who wants to learn about becoming a spy? Include **two** details from the selection in your answer.

_____
_____
_____
_____
_____
_____
_____
_____

Go on ▶

Directions: Read the selection and answer the questions.

Bill Gates

1   Bill Gates had a dream that changed the world. Born in Seattle, Washington, on October 28, 1955, Bill Gates grew up with his parents and his two sisters. As a teenager, Bill believed that computers would change everyone's life, and he wanted to be a part of it.

2   Bill Gates went to Lakeside School in Seattle. He was very smart and got straight As in school. After school and on weekends, he worked on what he loved best: computers. Sometimes he would forget to sleep and would work all night on the computer. He knew more about computers than most grown-ups.

3   When he was 13, Bill began writing computer programs[1] that told the computer what to do. Bill knew that computers could be used for things like helping kids with math problems, writing stories, drawing pictures, or playing games.

4   In 1973, Bill went to Harvard University as a freshman. In college, Bill began to write a computer language[2]. In 1975, Bill and his old school friend Paul Allen began a company called Microsoft. Bill believed that computers would one day be used by people at work, in schools, and in homes. He knew that people would use computers to help them do their work and to have fun.

5   Bill worked for six weeks with his friend Paul to write the first computer language program. Sometimes Bill would work sixteen to eighteen hours a day to get his work done. He found his old high school and college friends to help him in his company. Sometimes they brought sleeping bags to the office so they could work long hours to finish a job. Bill still works seventy to eighty hours a week at his job.

---

[1] computer program: a list of instructions that tells a computer how to do a job
[2] computer language: a vocabulary and set of rules for writing computer programs

Go on ▶

6   Bill Gates is one of the richest men in the world. He and his wife Melinda like to spend their money in ways that will help the world. They give billions of dollars to help improve[3] the learning and health of people all over the world. He even received an honorary knighthood from the Queen of England for his caring work.

7   Bill is a father of three children. When he is not working hard at his company, he likes to read or play golf.

---

[3] *improve: to make something better*

Go on ▶

11 What is most likely the author's purpose for writing the selection?

○ **A.** To describe to the reader how Bill Gates began Microsoft

○ **B.** To inform the reader about the life of Bill Gates

○ **C.** To demonstrate how to write computer language

12 How might the selection be useful to someone who wants to follow a dream? Include **two** details from the selection in your answer.

_____
_____
_____
_____
_____
_____
_____
_____

Go on ▶

13 Which sentence explains why Bill Gates founded Microsoft in the selection?

○ A. "As a teenager, Bill believed that computers would change everyone's life, and he wanted to be a part of it."

○ B. "After school and on weekends, he worked on what he loved best: computers."

○ C. "He knew more about computers than most grown-ups."

14 What is the main idea of the selection?

○ A. Bill Gates is one of the richest men on Earth.

○ B. Bill Gates works long and hard at Microsoft.

○ C. Bill Gates' work has had a great effect on our world.

15 According to the selection, which idea does the author of the selection discuss last?

○ A. Bill Gates wrote computer programs when he was 13.

○ B. Bill Gates works 70 to 80 hours a week at Microsoft.

○ C. Bill Gates worked 16 to 18 hours a day to start Microsoft.

Go on ▶

16 What is the meaning of the word *improve* in paragraph 6 of the selection?

○ A.   To make something stay the same

○ B.   To make something worse

○ C.   To make something better

17 Who would find the information in the selection most useful?

○ A.   A student researching a report on computer pioneers

○ B.   A student researching a report on computer languages

○ C.   A student researching a report on computer brands

Go on ▶

Directions: Read the story and answer the questions.

Good Morning, Sunshine

1   Annie woke up to a ray of sunlight on her face. She blinked her eyes and stretched her arms out from beneath her blankets. She couldn't believe it was morning already. It seemed as if she had just gone to sleep. Staring at the ceiling, she thought about her day and remembered what was going to happen in just two hours. Annie's stomach began to churn[1]. She sat up but fell back on her pillow. She closed her eyes again, secretly wishing it would all be over.

2   Her mother knocked and opened the bedroom door just a crack. She saw that Annie was awake. "Good morning, Sunshine. It's time to get up! You don't want to waste a second this morning."

3   But that's exactly what Annie wanted to do. Slowly, Annie pulled herself out of bed and looked around the room that was now hers. It was still a mess. Moving boxes were everywhere. Four white, empty walls stared back at her. Maybe it would be better when things were unpacked and put away. That's what her mom and dad kept telling her. Annie couldn't believe it would ever feel as comfortable as her old room.

4   The sunlight made it possible to study each wall. It had been too dark the night before. One wall had a tiny crack. It looked a little like a spider. "I'll never like a room with a spider crack," she thought to herself. Her mind was made up.

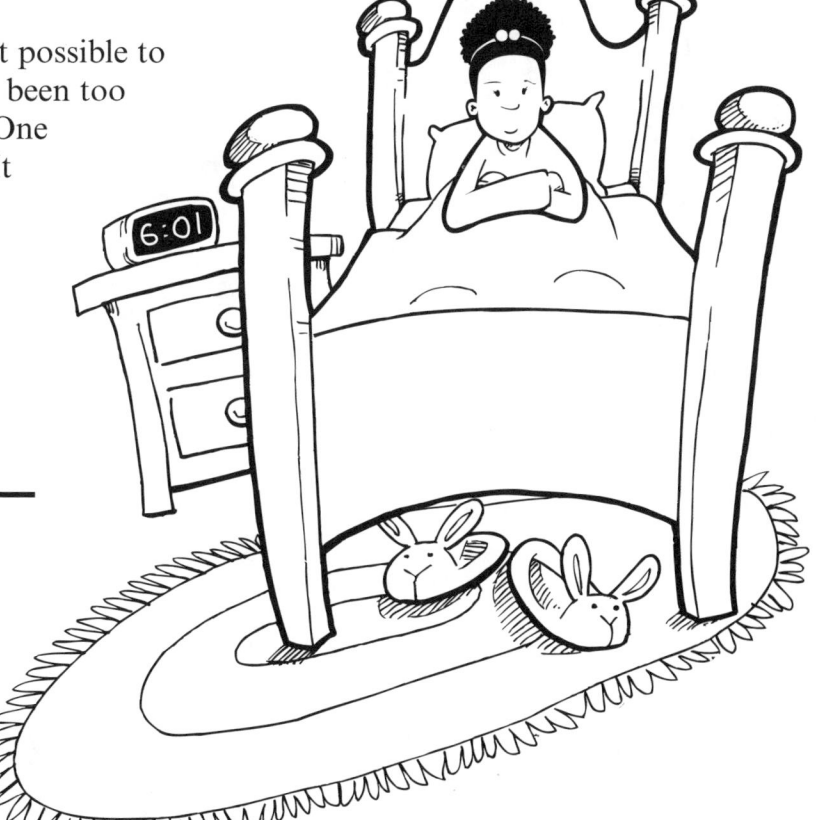

---

[1] churn: to move or stir with great force.

Go on ▶

5   A pair of jeans, a purple shirt, and some shoes—all new—were piled in the corner. Annie's mother had surprised her daughter with the gifts yesterday. Annie knew her mother was trying to make her feel better, but Annie thought she might be more comfortable in her old clothes. New clothes never felt as good as her old ones. Annie didn't even know where to start looking for her old favorites. She settled for the new stuff.

6   "Annie, I don't hear you moving. Are you up, Sunshine?"

7   "Why does she always call me that?" wondered Annie. It was a nickname Annie didn't like, but she had grown used to it. "She should call me Grumpy," Annie whispered to herself. "That's how I feel." She tied her shoes and combed her hair. Then, she walked into the hallway and down the stairs to greet a plate of pancakes.

8   "Oh Annie, you look great!" her mom smiled as she poured a tall glass of milk.

9   "Thanks," Annie said, but she didn't mean it. Around and around, she pushed her pancakes in circles on her plate. "How can I eat?" she thought. "My insides are tied in knots." Annie watched the clock count down the remaining moments of summer.

10 "Let's go, Annie," her dad said. "You're going to miss the bus."

Go on ▶

18 Based on the story, which word best describes Annie?

○ **A.** Happy

○ **B.** Scared

○ **C.** Pleased

19 Based on the information in the story, what do you predict Annie will do now that she is starting school in a new city?

○ **A.** She will fight with her parents and not go to school.

○ **B.** She will be nervous about meeting new people and fitting in.

○ **C.** She will be very excited to be in a new building and meet new people.

Go on ▶

20 What is the meaning of the word *unpacked* as it is used in paragraph 3 of the story?

- A. No longer packed
- B. Partly packed
- C. Not yet packed

21 What is the main idea of the story?

- A. Annie is happy and excited to be in a new house and starting classes at a new school.
- B. Annie is mean and nasty to her parents because they moved her to a new house and a new school.
- C. Annie is scared and nervous to be in a new house and starting classes at a new school.

Go on ▶

22 What do you think would be the best part of Annie moving to a new place? Include information from the story in your answer.

_____

_____

_____

_____

What do you think would be the worst part of Annie moving to a new place? Include information from the story in your answer.

_____

_____

_____

_____

Go on ▶

23 According to the story, where does the story take place?

- **A.** In Annie's old bedroom
- **B.** At Annie's school
- **C.** In Annie's new house

Go on ▶

Directions: Read the selection and answer the questions.

The Space Age

1   The Seattle World's Fair of 1962 was a peek into the 21st century[1]. It was the first world's fair to be held in the United States in over 20 years. The theme of the fair was "Century 21"; the focus of the fair was on space, the future, and science. Could you imagine seeing the Space Needle for the first time? Or one of the first home computers? Or the Monorail? These are all things that by the year 2000 seem "old fashioned."

2   The Seattle World's Fair was also known as The Century 21 Exposition[2]. The fair was about leaping into the future and seeing what new ideas lie ahead. The Fair was one of the most successful world's fairs in history.

3   The Space Needle was one of the symbols of the 1962 fair and is the most well known. At 600 feet high, the Space Needle has three elevators to carry passengers up to the Observation Deck, where you can see a bird's-eye view of Seattle. During the Seattle World's Fair, the Space Needle welcomed 2.3 million visitors.

4   The Space Needle was the tallest building west of the Mississippi at the time it was built. The building itself looks a flying saucer. It was one of the few buildings left standing after the fair ended.

5   The fair had many exhibitors. Exhibitors are people and companies that come to the fair and show new inventions. Some of these exhibitors presented new things like home computers. Home computers may be very common today, but in 1962 no one could believe that these machines would be so important to our future.

6   There were over 29 different countries that had displays at the fair. It was wonderful to see all of these different nations represented all in the same place. They brought with them the newest and best inventions to present to the world.

---

[1] *century: a period of 100 years, beginning with a year ending in 00 and runs through 99*
[2] *Exposition: a large public show*

7   The second most popular item at the World's Fair was the Monorail. In 1962, the price to ride the Monorail at the fair was 50 cents one-way, 75 cents round-trip for adults, and 35 cents one-way, 50 cents round-trip for children. What a deal! For just a few cents, you could ride on a high-speed monorail that was 1.2 miles long and would move people between downtown Seattle and the World's Fair site in 94 seconds.

8   The Monorail and the Space Needle were so well-known around the country that a four-cent postage stamp was put out with images of the Monorail and Space Needle on it.

9   Even though the fair has been gone for over 40 years, the people that went to the fair will never forget its sights and sounds. The Space Needle and the Monorail still remain as reminders of the fair of 1962. The exhibitors are now gone, but what they brought to the fair is still in many of the visitors' memories. It was a time when "the Space Age" seemed ages away.

Go on ▶

24 What does the author mean when he says "...where you can see a bird's-eye view of Seattle" in paragraph 3 of the selection?

○ A. A fuzzy view from high in the air

○ B. A clear view from ground level

○ C. A clear view of Seattle from high in the air

25 The author's purpose for writing the selection may have been to inform about the Seattle World's Fair. Support this purpose with **two** details from the selection.

_____

_____

_____

_____

_____

_____

_____

_____

Go on ▶

26 Which sentence best summarizes this selection?

- A. The Seattle World's Fair displayed visions of future scientific discoveries.
- B. The Seattle World's Fair was held so the Space Needle could be built.
- C. The Seattle World's Fair introduced the world to the Monorail.

27 Which sentence explains why a postage stamp with the Monorail and Space Needle on it was created?

- A. The Seattle World's Fair was one of the most popular of the 20th century.
- B. The Monorail and the Space Needle were well-known around the country.
- C. The fair had many exhibitors that were scientists and inventors.

Go on ▶

Seattle World's Fair 1962

1   The fair ran from April 21, 1962 to October 21, 1962. Attendance at the fair was 9,639,969 people. There were five main theme areas or "Worlds" at the fair. They were the World of Art, World of Century 21, World of Commerce, World of Entertainment, and World of Science. Symbols of the Fair included Man in Space and the Space Needle.

2   Some of the most popular activities at the Fair was people watching, riding the Monorail, and exploring the Space Needle. The Space Needle was built to withstand winds of up to 200 miles per hour. The elevators on the Space Needle travel at 10 miles per hour.

3   The high-speed Monorail was 1.2 miles long. More than 15,000 tons of steel were used in the construction of the Monorail. It traveled from downtown Seattle to the World's Fair in less than two minutes.

28 What word could the author have used in paragraph 3 instead of *construction*?

○ A. Building

○ B. Structure

○ C. Materials

29 Based on information in the selection, what would happen if a severe storm with winds of 150 mph hit Seattle?

○ A. The Space Needle would be destroyed.

○ B. The Space Needle would withstand the storm.

○ C. The elevators on the Space Needle would stop.

Go on ▶

30 The author of The Space Age states "The theme of the fair was 'Century 21'; the focus of the fair was on space, the future, and science." Include **two** examples from Seattle World's Fair that show how space was a theme of the fair.

_____

_____

_____

_____

_____

_____

_____

_____

STOP

Mathematics

Introduction

In the Mathematics Assessment of the Measurements of Student Progress (MSP), you will be asked questions to test the knowledge you have learned so far in school. These questions are based on the mathematical skills you have been taught in school through third grade. The questions you answer are not meant to confuse or trick you, but are written so you have the best opportunity to show what you know about mathematics.

The *Show What You Know® on the MSP for Grade 3, Student Workbook* includes a Mathematics Tutorial that will help you practice your test-taking skills. Following the Mathematics Tutorial is a full-length Mathematics Assessment. Both the Mathematics Tutorial and the Mathematics Assessment have been created to model the Grade 3 Measurements of Student Progress for Mathematics.

About the Mathematics MSP

The Grade 3 Mathematics Assessment will test Content (numbers, operations, algebra, geometry/measurement, data/statistics/probability) as well as Process (reasoning, problem solving, and communication). The Mathematics Assessment is given in one session.

For the Mathematics Assessment there are three different types of questions: multiple choice, completion, and short answer. Dictionaries, thesauruses, and scratch paper are not allowed on the Mathematics Assessment.

Scoring

On the MSP for Grade 3 Mathematics Assessment, each multiple-choice item is worth one point. Short-answer items will be scored on a scale of zero to two points. The scoring criteria will focus on the understanding of mathematical ideas, information, and solutions, and will disregard conventions of writing (complete sentences, usage/grammar, spelling, capitals, punctuation, and paragraphing), as long as the wording of the response does not interfere with the mathematical communication.

Typical Distribution of Score Points by Item Type*

Type	Number of Items	Total Possible Points
Multiple Choice	22	22
Short Answer	8	16
Total	30	38

*2009 testing information

Glossary

addend: Numbers added together to give a sum. For example, 2 + 7 = 9. The numbers 2 and 7 are addends.

addition: An operation joining two or more sets where the result is the whole.

a.m.: The hours from midnight to noon; from Latin words *ante meridiem* meaning "before noon."

analyze: To break down information into parts so that it may be more easily understood.

angle: A figure formed by two rays that meet at the same end point called a vertex. Angles can be obtuse, acute, right, or straight.

area: The number of square units needed to cover a region. The most common abbreviation for area is *A*.

Associative Property of Addition: The grouping of addends can be changed and the sum will be the same. Example: (3 + 1) + 2 = 6; 3 + (1 + 2) = 6.

Associative Property of Multiplication: The grouping of factors can be changed and the product will be the same. Example: (3 x 2) x 4 = 24; 3 x (2 x 4) = 24.

attribute: A characteristic or distinctive feature.

average: A number found by adding two or more quantities together and then dividing the sum by the number of quantities. For example, in the set {9, 5, 3}, the average is 6: 9 + 5 + 4 = 18; 18 ÷ 3 = 6. *See mean.*

axes: Plural of axis. Perpendicular lines used as reference lines in a coordinate system or graph; traditionally, the horizontal axis (*x*-axis) represents the independent variable and the vertical axis (*y*-axis) represents the dependent variable.

bar graph: A graph using bars to show data.

capacity: The amount an object holds when filled.

chart: A way to show information, such as in a graph or table.

circle: A closed, curved line made up of points that are all the same distance from a point inside called the center. Example: A circle with center point *P* is shown below.

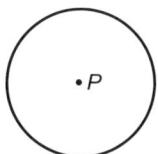

circle graph: Sometimes called a pie chart; a way of representing data that shows the fractional part or percentage of an overall set as an appropriately sized wedge of a circle. Example:

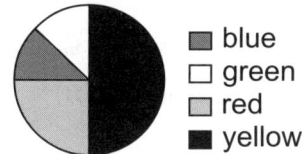

circumference: The boundary line or perimeter of a circle; also, the length of the perimeter of a circle. Example:

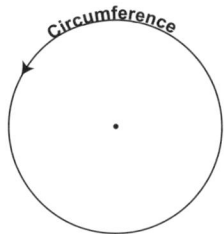

Commutative Property of Addition: Numbers can be added in any order and the sum will be the same. Example: 3 + 4 = 4 + 3.

Commutative Property of Multiplication: Numbers can be multiplied in any order and the product will be the same. Example: 3 x 6 = 6 x 3.

compare: To look for similarities and differences. For example, is one number greater than, less than, or equal to another number?

conclusion: A statement that follows logically from other facts.

Glossary

cone: A solid figure with a circle as its base and a curved surface that meets at a point.

cones

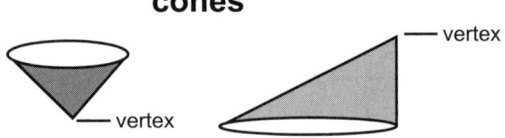

congruent figures: Figures that have the same shape and size.

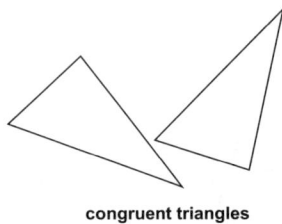

congruent triangles

cube: A solid figure with six faces that are congruent (equal) squares.

cylinder: A solid figure with two circular bases that are congruent (equal) and parallel to each other connected by a curved lateral surface.

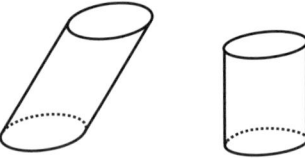

data: Information that is collected.

decimal number: A number expressed in base 10, such as 39.356, where each digit's value is determined by multiplying it by some power of 10.

denominator: The bottom number in a fraction.

diagram: A drawing that represents a mathematical situation.

difference: The answer when subtracting two numbers.

distance: The amount of space between two points.

dividend: A number in a division problem that is divided. Dividend ÷ divisor = quotient. Example: In 15 ÷ 3 = 5, 15 is the dividend.

$$\text{divisor}\overline{)\text{dividend}}^{\text{quotient}} \qquad 3\overline{)15}^{\,5}$$

divisible: Can be divided by another number without leaving a remainder. Example: 12 is divisible by 3 because 12 ÷ 3 is an integer, namely 4.

division: An operation that tells how many equal groups there are or how many are in each group.

divisor: The number by which another number is divided. Example: In 15 ÷ 3 = 5, 3 is the divisor.

$$\text{divisor}\overline{)\text{dividend}}^{\text{quotient}} \qquad 3\overline{)15}^{\,5}$$

edge: The line segment where two faces of a solid figure meet.

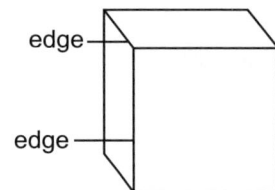

equality: Two or more sets of values that are equal.

equation: A number sentence that says two expressions are equal (=). Example: 4 + 8 = 6 + 6.

equivalent fractions: Two fractions with equal values.

estimate: To find an approximate value or measurement of something without exact calculation.

even number: A whole number that has a 0, 2, 4, 6, or 8 in the ones place. A number that is a multiple of 2. Examples: 0, 4, and 678 are even numbers.

expanded form: A number written as the sum of the values of its digits. Example: 546 = 500 + 40 + 6.

Glossary

expression: A combination of variables, numbers, and symbols that represent a mathematical relationship.

face: The sides of a solid figure. For example, a cube has six faces that are all squares. The pyramid below has five faces—four triangles and one square.

fact family: A group of related facts using the same numbers. Example: 5 + 8 = 13; 13 − 8 = 5.

factor: One of two or more numbers that are multiplied together to give a product. Example: In 3 × 4 = 12, 3 and 4 are factors of 12.

figure: A geometric figure is a set of points and/or lines in 2 or 3 dimensions.

flip (reflection): The change in a position of a figure that is the result of picking it up and turning it over. Example: Reversing a "b" to a "d."
Tipping a "p" to a "b" or a "b" to a "p" as shown below:

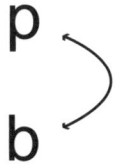

fraction: A symbol, such as $\frac{2}{8}$ or $\frac{5}{3}$, used to name a part of a whole, a part of a set, or a location on the number line. Examples:

$$\frac{\text{numerator}}{\text{denominator}} = \frac{\text{dividend}}{\text{divisor}}$$

$$\frac{\text{\# of parts under consideration}}{\text{\# of parts in a set}}$$

function machine: Applies a function rule to a set of numbers, which determines a corresponding set of numbers.
Example: Input 9 → Rule × 7 → Output 63. If you apply the function rule "multiply by 7" to the values 5, 7, and 9, the corresponding values are:
$$5 \rightarrow 35$$
$$7 \rightarrow 49$$
$$9 \rightarrow 63$$

graph: A "picture" showing how certain facts are related to each other or how they compare to one another. Some examples of types of graphs are line graphs, pie charts, bar graphs, scatterplots, and pictographs.

grid: A pattern of regularly spaced horizontal and vertical lines on a plane that can be used to locate points and graph equations.

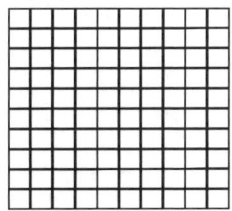

hexagon: A six-sided polygon. The total measure of the angles within a hexagon is 720°.

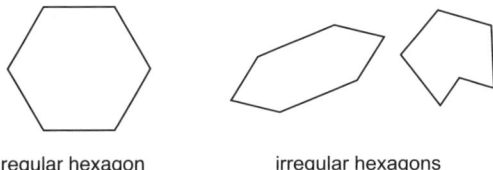

regular hexagon   irregular hexagons

impossible event: An event that can never happen.

integer: Any number, positive or negative, that is a whole number distance away from zero on a number line, in addition to zero. Specifically, an integer is any number in the set {. . .-3,-2,-1, 0, 1, 2, 3. . .}. Examples of integers include: 1, 5, 273, -2, -35, and -1,375.

intersecting lines: Lines that cross at a point. Examples:

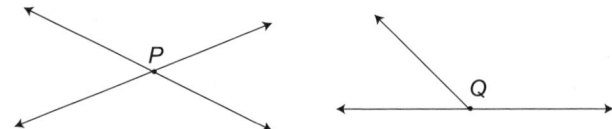

Glossary

isosceles triangle: A triangle with at least two sides the same length.

justify: To prove or show to be true or valid using logic and/or evidence.

key: An explanation of what each symbol represents in a pictograph.

kilometer (km): A metric unit of length: 1 kilometer = 1,000 meters.

line: A straight path of points that goes on forever in both directions.

line graph: A graph that uses a line or a curve to show how data changes over time.

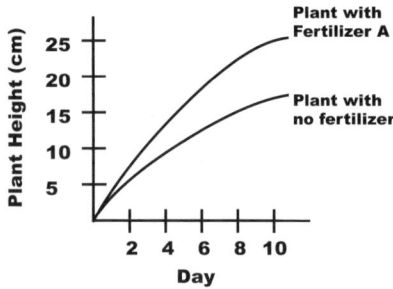

line of symmetry: A line on which a figure can be folded into two parts so that the parts match exactly.

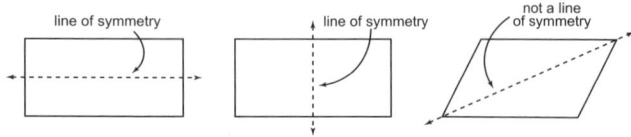

liter (L): A metric unit of capacity: 1 liter = 1,000 milliliters.

mass: The amount of matter an object has.

mean: Also called arithmetic average. A number found by adding two or more quantities together, and then dividing the sum by the number of quantities. For example, in the set {9, 5, 3} the mean is 6: 9 + 5 + 4 = 18; 18 ÷ 3 = 6. *See average.*

median: The middle number when numbers are put in order from least to greatest or from greatest to least. For example, in the set of numbers 6, 7, 8, 9, 10, the number 8 is the median (middle) number.

meter (m): A metric unit of length: 1 meter = 100 centimeters.

method: A systematic way of accomplishing a task.

mixed number: A number consisting of a whole number and a fraction. Example: $6\frac{2}{3}$.

mode: The number or numbers that occur most often in a set of data. Example: The mode of {1, 3, 4, 5, 5, 7, 9} is 5.

multiple: A product of a number and any other whole number. Examples: {2, 4, 6, 8, 10, 12,...} are multiples of 2.

multiplication: An operation on two numbers that tells how many in all. The first number is the number of sets and the second number tells how many in each set.

number line: A line that shows numbers in order using a scale. Equal intervals are marked and usually labeled on the number line.

number sentence: An expression of a relationship between quantities as an equation or an inequality. Examples: 7 + 7 = 8 + 6; 13 < 92; 56 + 4 > 59.

numerator: The top number in a fraction.

octagon: An eight-sided polygon. The total measure of the angles within an octagon is 1080°.

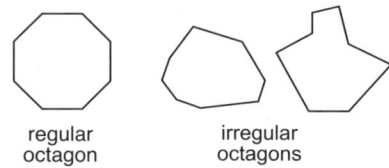

odd number: A whole number that has 1, 3, 5, 7, or 9 in the ones place. An odd number is not divisible by 2. Examples: The numbers 53 and 701 are odd numbers.

operation: A mathematical process that combines numbers; basic operations of arithmetic include addition, subtraction, multiplication, and division.

order: To arrange numbers from the least to greatest or from the greatest to least.

Glossary

ordered pair: Two numbers inside a set of parentheses separated by a comma that are used to name a point on a coordinate grid.

parallel lines: Lines in the same plane that never intersect.

parallelogram: A quadrilateral in which opposite sides are parallel.

pattern: An arrangement of numbers, pictures, etc., in an organized and predictable way. Examples: 3, 6, 9, 12, or ® 0 ® 0 ® 0.

pentagon: A five-sided polygon. The total measure of the angles within a pentagon is 540°.

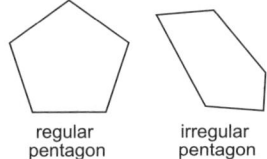

perimeter: The distance around a figure.

perpendicular lines: Two lines that intersect to form a right angle (90 degrees).

pictograph: A graph that uses pictures or symbols to represent similar data. The value of each picture is interpreted by a "key" or "legend."

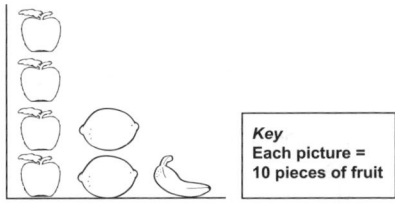

place value: The value given to the place a digit has in a number.
Example: In the number 135, the 1 is in the hundreds place so it represents 100 (1 x 100), the 3 is in the tens place so it represents 30 (3 x 10), and the 5 is in the ones place so it represents 5 (5 x 1).

p.m.: The hours from noon to midnight; from the Latin words *post meridiem* meaning "after noon."

point: An exact position often marked by a dot.

polygon: A closed figure made up of straight line segments.

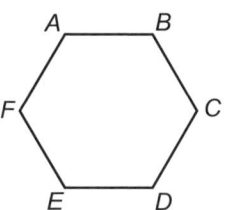

ABCDEF is a polygon.

possible event: An event that might or might not happen.

predict: To tell what you believe may happen in the future.

prediction: A description of what may happen before it happens.

probability: The likelihood that something will happen.

product: The answer to a multiplication problem. Example: In 3 x 4 = 12, 12 is the product.

pyramid: A solid figure in which the base is a polygon and faces are triangles with a common point called a vertex.

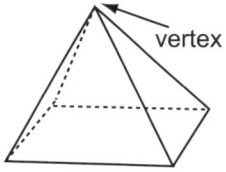

quadrilateral: A four-sided polygon. Rectangles, squares, parallelograms, rhombi, and trapezoids are all quadrilaterals. The total measure of the angles within a quadrilateral is 360°. Example: ABCD is a quadrilateral.

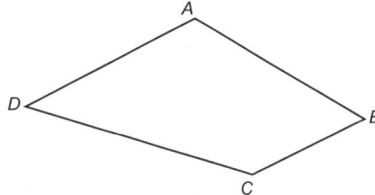

questionnaire: A set of questions for a survey.

Glossary

quotient: The answer in a division problem. Dividend ÷ divisor = quotient. Example: In 15 ÷ 3 = 5, 5 is the quotient.

range: The difference between the least number and the greatest number in a data set. For example, in the set {4, 7, 10, 12, 36, 7, 2}, the range is 34; the greatest number (36) minus the least number (2): (36 − 2 = 34).

rectangle: A quadrilateral with four right angles. A square is one example of a rectangle.

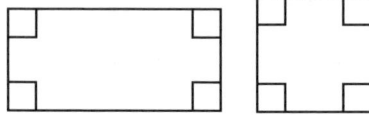

reflection: The change in the position of a figure that is the result of picking it up and turning it over. *See flip.*

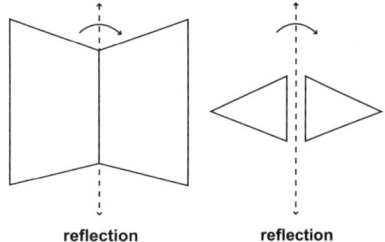

remainder: The number that is left over after dividing. Example: In 31 ÷ 7 = 4 R 3, the 3 is the remainder.

represent: To present clearly; describe; show.

rhombus: A quadrilateral with opposite sides parallel and all sides the same length. A square is one kind of rhombus.

right angle: An angle that forms a square corner and measures 90 degrees.

right triangle: A triangle having one right angle. *See angle and triangle.*

rounding: Replacing an exact number with a number that tells about how much or how many to the nearest ten, hundred, thousand, and so on. Example: 52 rounded to the nearest 10 is 50.

rule: A procedure; a prescribed method; a way of describing the relationship between two sets of numbers. Example: In the following data, the rule is to add 3:

Input	Output
3	6
5	8
9	12

ruler: A straight-edged instrument used for measuring the lengths of objects. A ruler usually measures smaller units of length, such as inches or centimeters.

scale: The numbers that show the size of the units used on a graph.

sequence: A set of numbers arranged in a special order or pattern.

set: A group made up of numbers, figures, or parts.

side: A line segment connected to other segments to form the boundary of a polygon.

similar: A description for figures that have the same shape.

slide (translation): The change in the position of a figure that moves up, down, or sideways. Example: scooting a book on a table.

solids: Figures in three dimensions.

solve: To find the solution to an equation or problem; finding the values of unknown variables that will make a true mathematical statement.

sphere: A solid figure in the shape of a ball. Example: a basketball is a sphere.

Glossary

square: A rectangle with congruent (equal) sides. *See rectangle.*

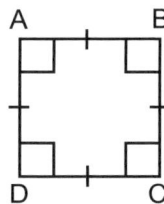

square number: The product of a number multiplied by itself. Example: 49 is a square number (7 x 7 = 49).

square unit: A square with sides 1 unit long, used to measure area.

standard form: A way to write a number showing only its digits. Example: 2,389.

standard units of measure: Units of measure commonly used; generally classified in the U.S. as the customary system or the metric system:

> **Customary System:**
> **Length**
> 1 foot (ft) = 12 inches (in)
> 1 yard (yd) = 3 feet or 36 inches
> 1 mile (mi) = 1,760 yards or 5,280 feet
>
> **Weight**
> 16 ounces (oz) = 1 pound (lb)
> 2,000 pounds = 1 ton (t)
>
> **Capacity**
> 1 pint (pt) = 2 cups (c)
> 1 quart (qt) = 2 pints
> 1 gallon (gal) = 4 quarts

> **Metric System:**
> **Length**
> 1 centimeter (cm) = 10 millimeters (mm)
> 1 decimeter (dm) = 10 centimeters
> 1 meter (m) = 100 centimeters
> 1 kilometer (km) = 1,000 meters
>
> **Weight**
> 1,000 milligrams (mg) = 1 gram (g)
> 1,000 grams (g) = 1 kilogram (kg)
> 1,000 kilograms (kg) = 1 tonne (metric ton)
>
> **Capacity**
> 1 liter (l) = 1,000 milliliters (ml)

strategy: A plan used in problem solving, such as looking for a pattern, drawing a diagram, working backward, etc.

subtraction: The operation that finds the difference between two numbers.

sum: The answer when adding two or more addends. Addend + Addend = Sum.

summary: A series of statements containing evidence, facts, and/or procedures that support a result.

survey: A way to collect data by asking a certain number of people the same question and recording their answers.

symmetry: A figure has line symmetry if it can be folded along a line so that both parts match exactly. A figure has radial or rotational symmetry if, after a rotation of less than 360°, it is indistinguishable from its former image.

Z unrotated   Z rotated 90°   Z rotated 180°

The letter Z has 180° radial or rotational symmetry.

table: A method of displaying data in rows and columns.

temperature: A measure of hot or cold in degrees.

translation (slide): A change in the position of a figure that moves it up, down, or sideways.

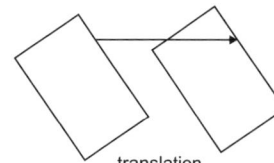

translation

Glossary

triangle: A polygon with three sides. The sum of the angles of a triangle is always equal to 180°.

turn: The change in the position of a figure that moves it around a point. Also called a rotation. Example: The hands of a clock turn around the center of the clock in a clockwise direction.

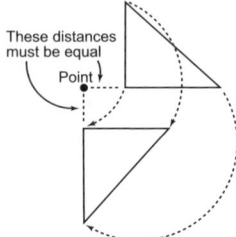

unlikely event: An event that probably will not happen.

vertex: The point where two rays meet to form an angle or where the sides of a polygon meet, or the point where 3 or more edges meet in a solid figure.

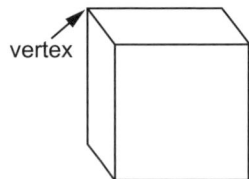

whole number: An integer in the set {0, 1, 2, 3 . . .}. In other words, a whole number is any number used when counting in addition to zero.

word forms: The number written in words. Examples: 546 is "five hundred forty-six."

Examples of Common Two-Dimensional Geometric Shapes

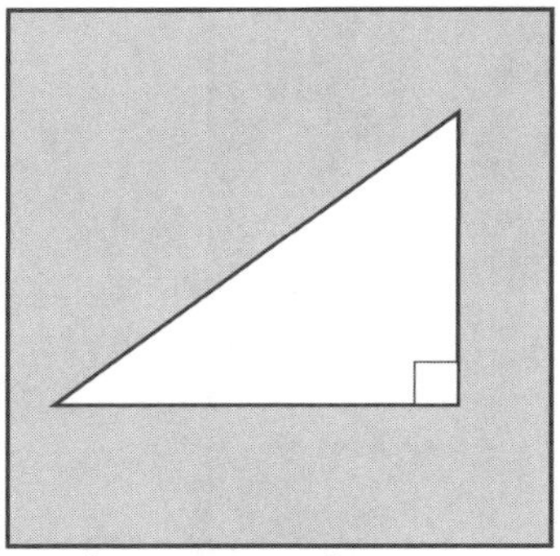

Right Triangle

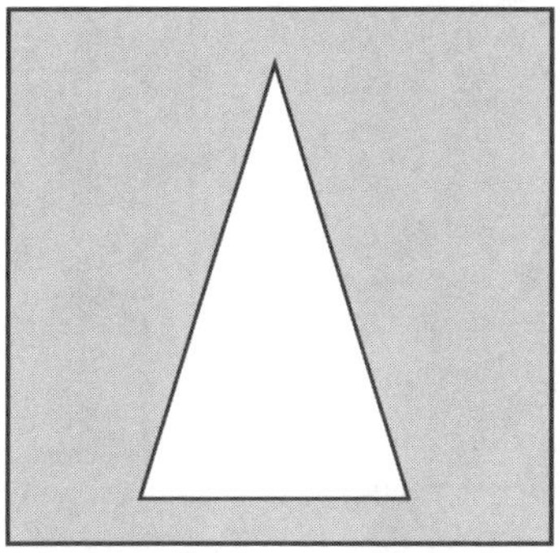

Isosceles Triangle

Equilateral Triangle

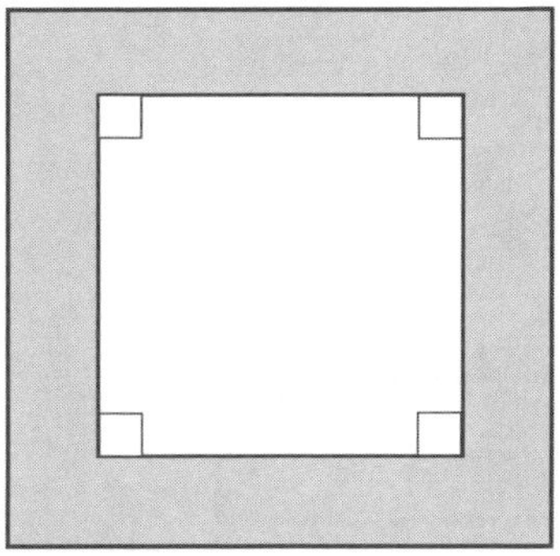

Square

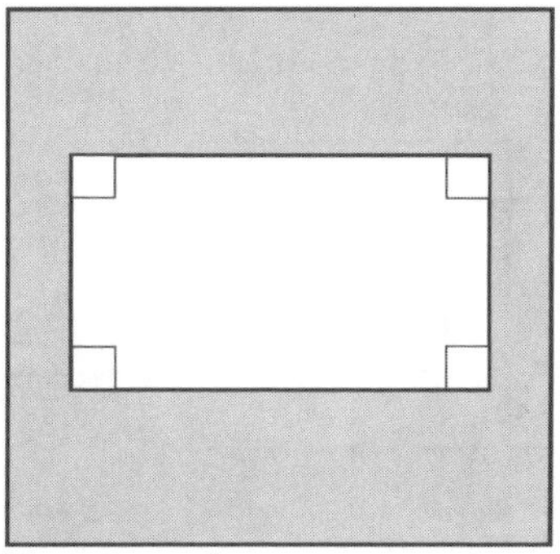

Rectangle

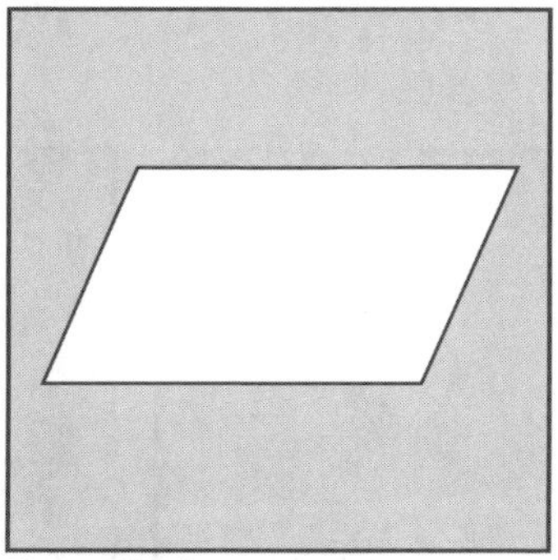

Parallelogram

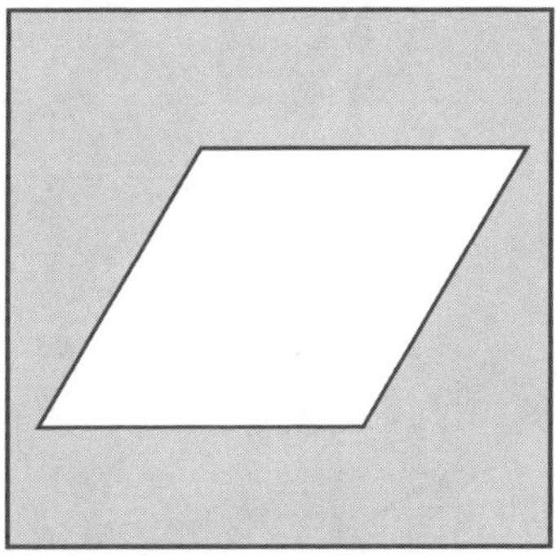

Rhombus

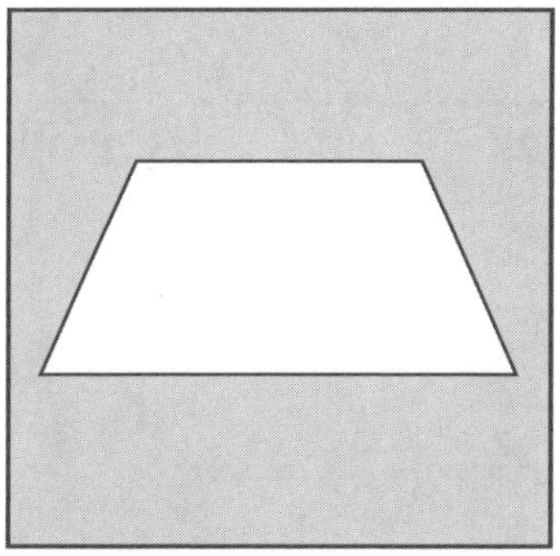

Trapezoid

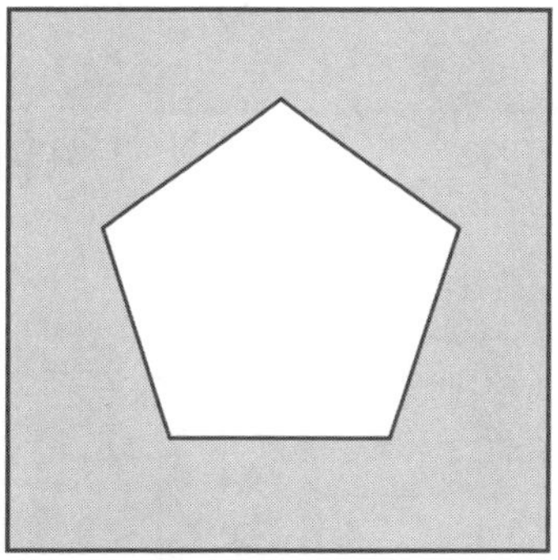

Pentagon

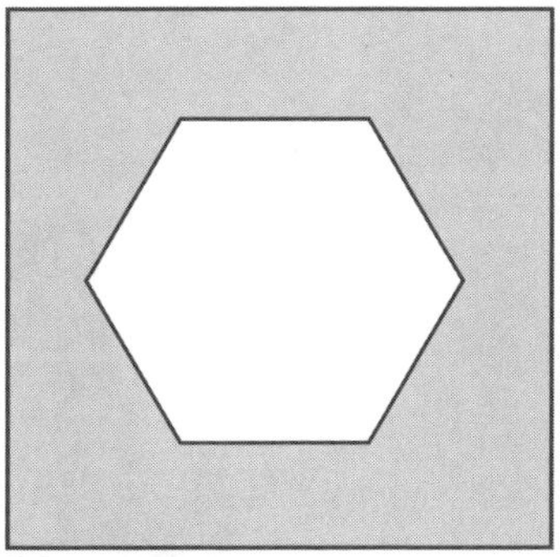

Hexagon

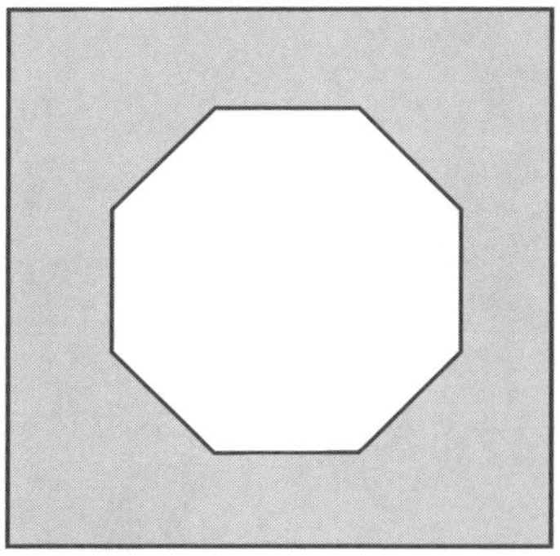

Octagon

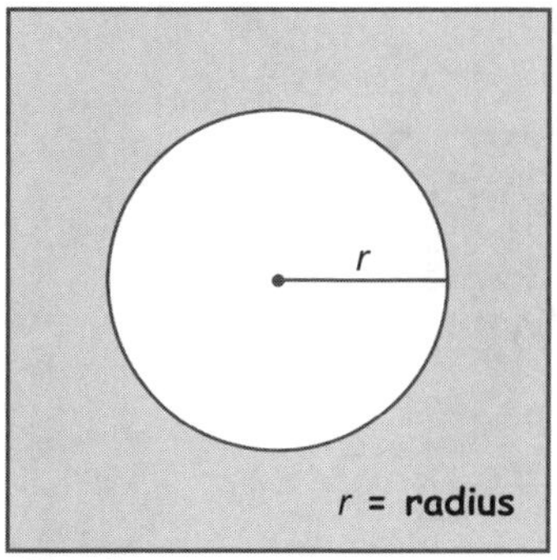

Circle (r = radius)

Examples of How Lines Interact

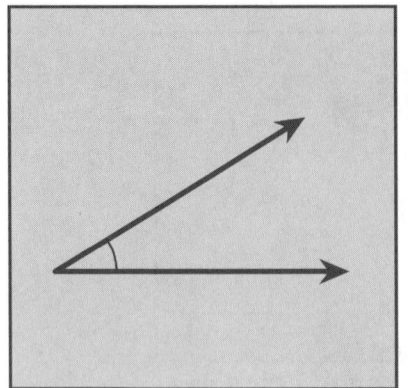
Acute Angle

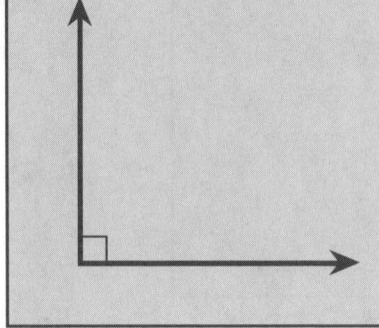
Right Angle

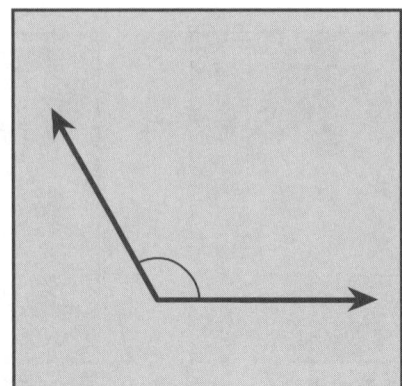
Obtuse Angle

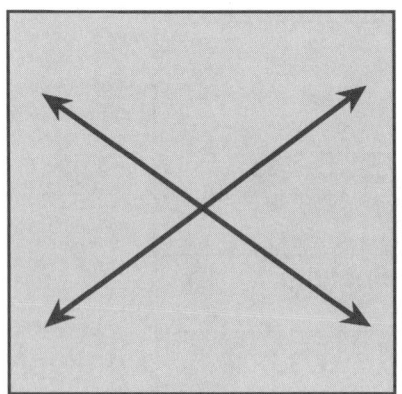
Intersecting

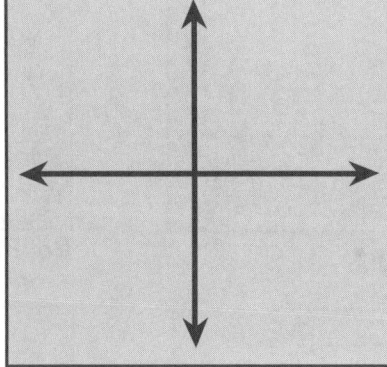
Perpendicular

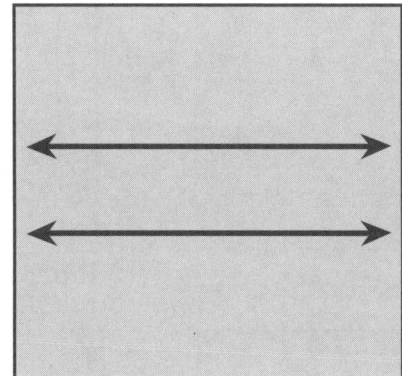
Parallel

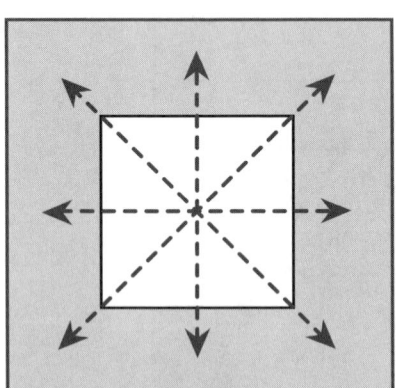
Lines of Symmetry

Examples of Common Types of Graphs

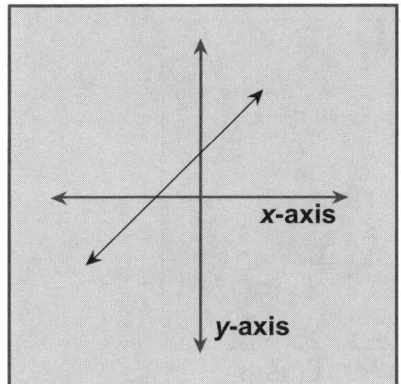
Line Graph

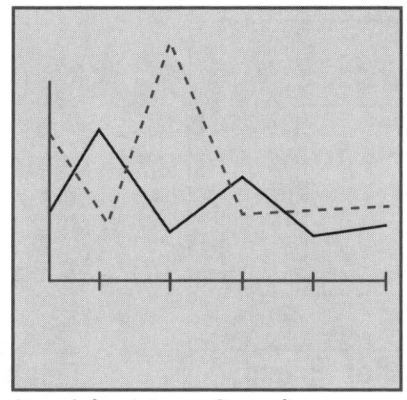
Double Line Graph

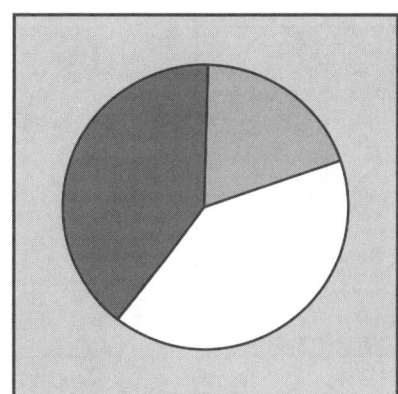
Pie Chart

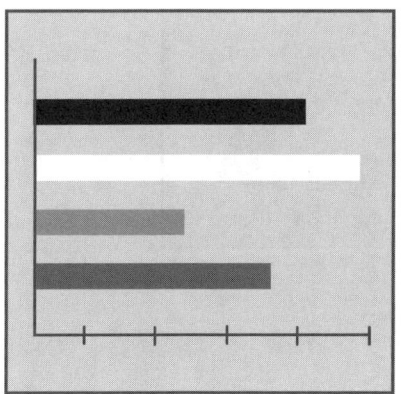
Bar Graph

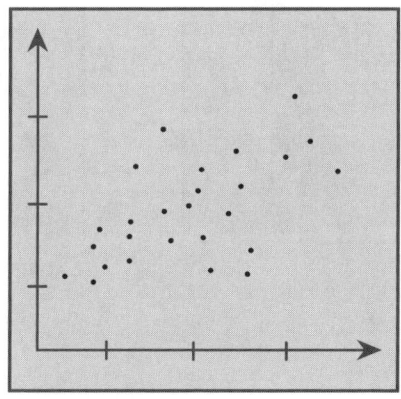
Scatterplot

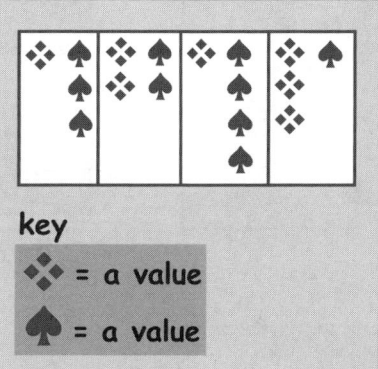
Pictograph

Examples of Common Three-Dimensional Objects

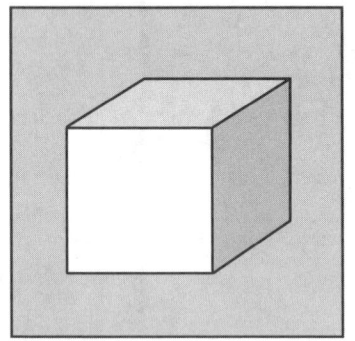
Cube

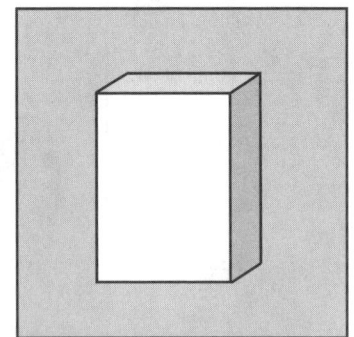
Rectangular Prism

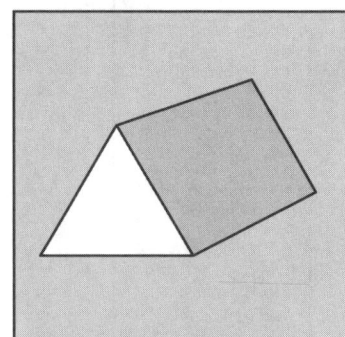
Triangular Prism

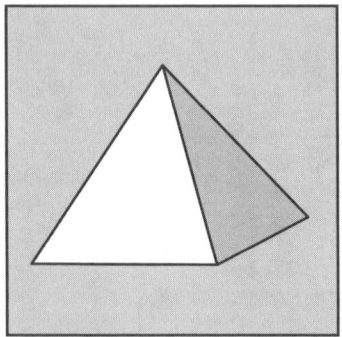
Pyramid

Cylinder

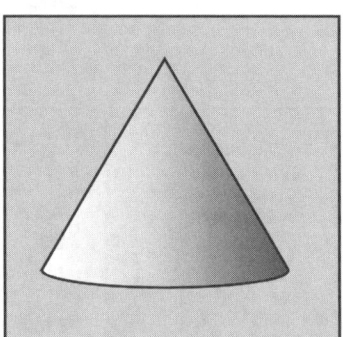
Cone

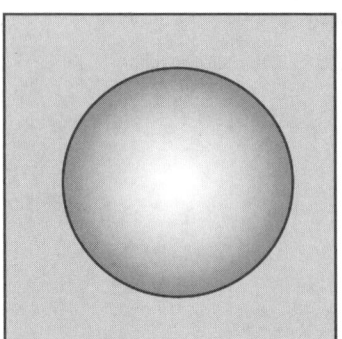
Sphere

Examples of Object Movement

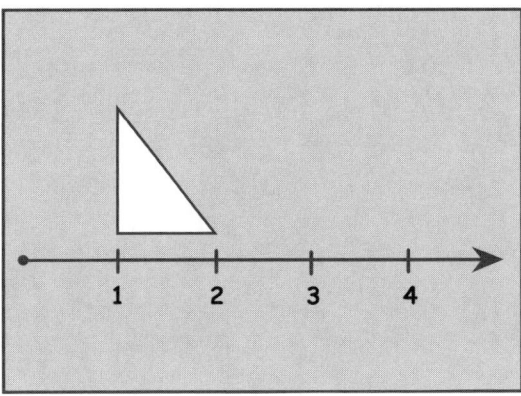
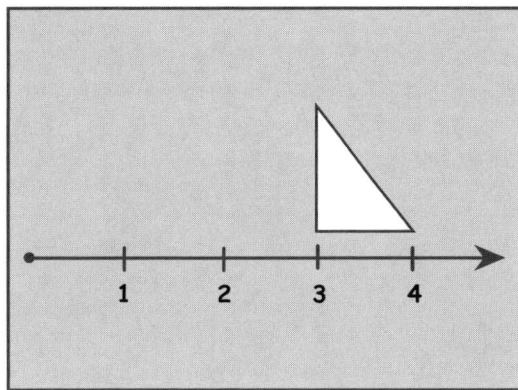

Translation

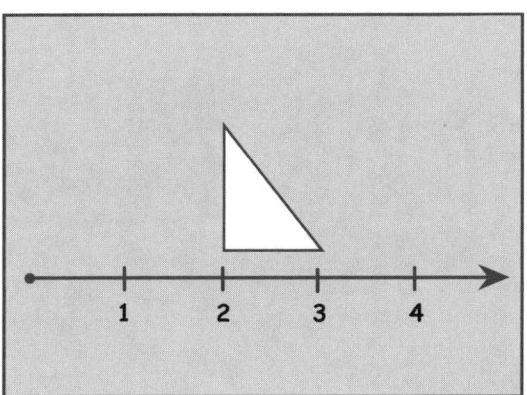
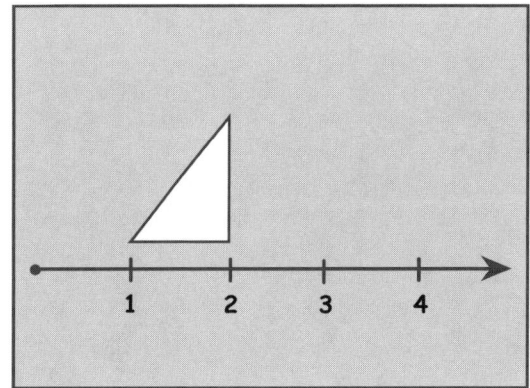

Reflection

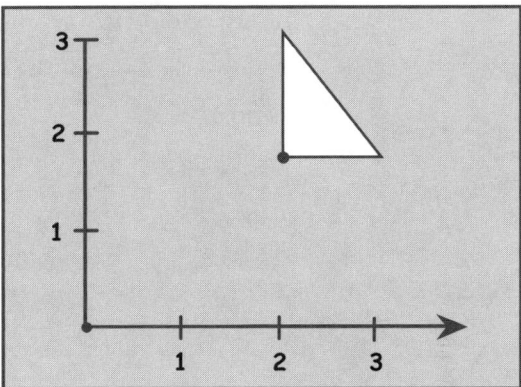
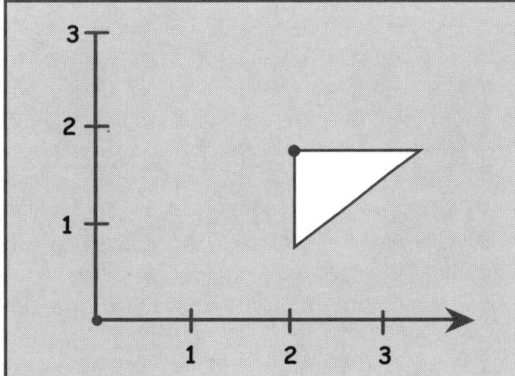

Rotation

This page left intentionally blank.

Mathematics Tutorial

The Mathematics Tutorial is made up of multiple-choice questions, completion items, and short-answer questions. These questions show you how the skills you have learned in Mathematics class may be tested on the Mathematics MSP. The questions also give you a chance to practice your skills. If you have trouble with an area, talk with a parent or teacher.

Read each question carefully. If you do not know an answer, you may skip the question and come back to it later.

When you finish, check your answers.

Directions for Mathematics Tutorial

Today you will take the Mathematics Tutorial.

Directions to the Student

There are several different types of questions on this tutorial:
1. Some questions will ask you to choose the best answer from three answer choices. These items are worth one point.

2. Some questions will ask you to write your answer in an answer box.

    - Some of these questions are short. They ask you to write only an answer, for example, a single number or one or two words.

    - Others ask for more details or more thinking. They ask you to write an answer, to explain your thinking using words, numbers, or pictures, or to show the steps you used to solve a problem. These items are worth two points.

Here are some important things to remember as you take this tutorial:
1. Read each question carefully and think about the answer.

2. If answer choices are given, choose the best answer by filling in the circle in front of your answer.

3. If an answer box is provided, write your answer neatly and clearly **inside** the box and show all your work. Cross out or erase any work you do not want as part of your answer. **Do not use scratch paper.**

3. Use only a **No. 2 pencil,** not a mechanical pencil or pen, to write your answers directly in your test booklet. If you do not have a No. 2 pencil, ask your teacher to give you one.

5. You should have plenty of time to finish every question on the test. If you do not know the answer to a question, go on to the next question. You can come back to that question later.

6. If you finish early, you may check your work in this test section **only**. Do **not** look ahead to the questions in the next sections.

7. When you reach the word **STOP** in your booklet, do not go on until you are told to turn the page.

Go on ▶

Show What You Know® on the MSP for Grade 3   Mathematics Tutorial

Sample Questions

To help you understand how to answer the test questions, look at the sample test questions below. They are included to show you what the questions in the test are like and how to mark or write your answers.

Multiple-Choice Sample Question

For this type of question you will select the answer and fill in the circle next to it.

1 William's basketball team is having a pizza party. There are **eight** players on the team. **Three** pizzas with **eight** slices each have been ordered. Each player will get an equal amount of pizza.

How much pizza will each player get?

○ A. 1 slice

● B. 3 slices

○ C. 6 slices

For this sample question, the correct answer is B; therefore, the circle next to B is filled in.

Completion Item Sample Question

For this type of question you will provide a short answer such as a single number or one or two words.

2 Samantha has 50¢. After she bought a gumball, she had 25¢ left.

• Write how much the gumball cost.

How much did the gumball cost? 25¢

Go on ▶

Copying is Prohibited   Student Workbook   113

Short-Answer Sample Question

For this type of question you will write and explain your answer using words, numbers, or pictures.

3 Kathy has two packs of gum with five pieces in each pack. She wants to share the gum equally with her friends, Stephanie and Missy. How many pieces of gum will each of the girls have if they are only given whole pieces of gum? Show your work using words, numbers, and/or pictures.

Kathy   *Stephanie*   *Missy*
| | | | | / | | |

3 + 3 + 3 + 1 piece of gum left over = 10

2 packs of gum with 5 pieces each

5 + 5 = 10 pieces of gum

Each girl will have __3__ pieces of gum.

Go on ▶

1 Rebecca and Carl each collect cartoon trading cards. They have two different types of cards: black-dog cards and red-dog cards. They counted the cards. Rebecca has 122 black-dog cards and 64 red-dog cards. Carl has 142 black-dog cards and 124 red-dog cards.

What is the order of numbers from **greatest** to **least**?

- A. 124, 142, 122, 64
- B. 142, 124, 122, 64
- C. 122, 124, 142, 64

2 For three weeks, the students at Kenwood School sold tickets to their spring play.

The first week they sold 124 tickets; the second week they sold 96 tickets; and the third week they sold 153 tickets.

Rounding to the **nearest hundred**, about how many tickets did the students sell altogether?

- A. 200
- B. 300
- C. 400

Go on▶

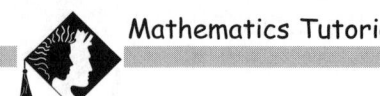

3 Lindsay had 72¢. After she bought an apple, she had 19¢ left.

• Write how much the apple costs.

How much did the apple cost? _____

4 Katie has a collection of 32 rocks. Jeanette has 15 rocks in her collection.

Use **estimation** to decide how many rocks are in both collections.

○ **A.** 40 rocks

○ **B.** 50 rocks

○ **C.** 60 rocks

Go on ▶

5 Corey is collecting shells at the beach. He finds 8 shells in the morning. By dinnertime, he has 26 shells.

How many shells did he collect in the afternoon?

• Write an equation to find the answer.

• Solve the equation to find the number of shells.

How many shells did he collect in the afternoon? _____

Go on ▶

6 Devon has 7 flowerpots. She wants to plant 4 flower seeds in each pot.

How many seeds will Devon need?

○ **A.** 21 seeds

○ **B.** 24 seeds

○ **C.** 28 seeds

Go on ▶

7 Mr. Patel drew enough stars on the board to represent 18 ÷ 3 = 6.

Which picture did the students in Mr. Patel's class pick?

○ A.

○ B.

○ C.

Go on ▶

8 Angelina has 20 pennies. She wants to give each of her **five** friends an equal amount of pennies.

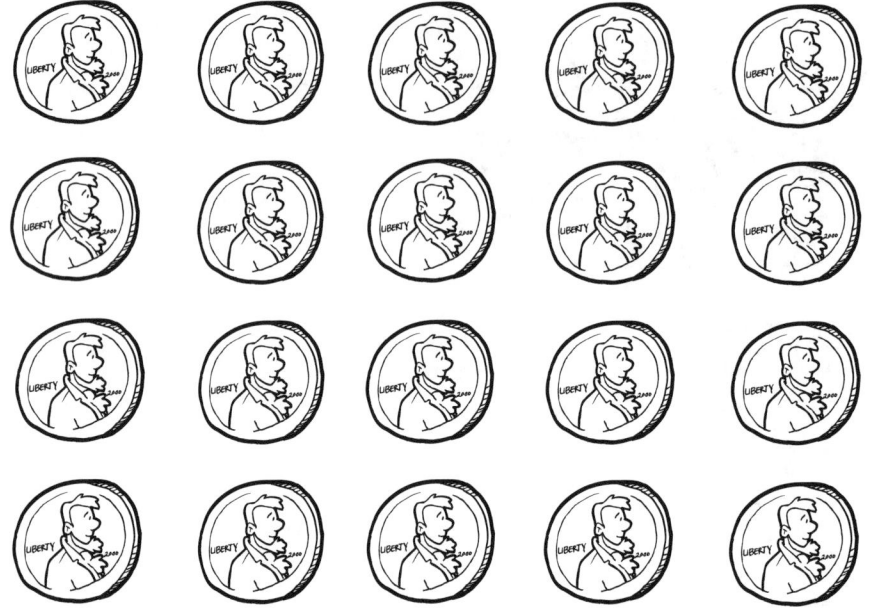

How many pennies does Angelina give to each of her friends?

○ A. 2

○ B. 4

○ C. 5

9 Look at the equation.

$$4 \times \square = 0$$

Which of the numbers below will make this number sentence **true**?

○ **A.** 0

○ **B.** 1

○ **C.** 2

Go on ▶

10 Jean-Claude bought crayons.

Crazy Crayons are packaged in boxes of 5 crayons per box. Jean-Claude purchased 3 boxes.

What is the **total** number of crayons Jean-Claude bought?

Show your work using words, numbers, or pictures.

What is the total number of crayons Jean-Claude bought? _____

Go on ▶

11 Look at the equation below.

$$6 \div 2 = 3$$

Create a situation using pictures or words that represents this equation.

Go on ▶

12 Owen sold 11 boxes of popcorn for his Boy Scout troop. Each box of popcorn cost $6.00.

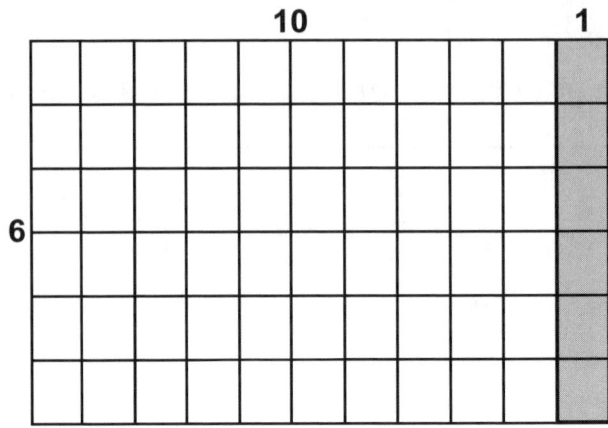

What is the **total** amount Owen made selling popcorn?

○ **A.** $60.00

○ **B.** $61.00

○ **C.** $66.00

13 Kris has 4 rosebushes in her yard. She picks 3 roses from each bush. She wants to put the roses into 2 vases, with the same number of roses in each vase.

How many roses will she put into each vase?

Show how you got your answer using words, numbers, or pictures.

How many roses will she put into each vase? _____

Go on ▶

14 Kate drew stars on the classroom chalkboard and shaded in a portion of them.

Which of the fractions shows the stars that Kate shaded?

○ A. $\frac{1}{4}$

○ B. $\frac{1}{3}$

○ C. $\frac{3}{4}$

Go on ▶

15 Sean ate $\frac{1}{4}$ of the cheese pizza and Trevor ate $\frac{1}{6}$ of the meatball pizza.

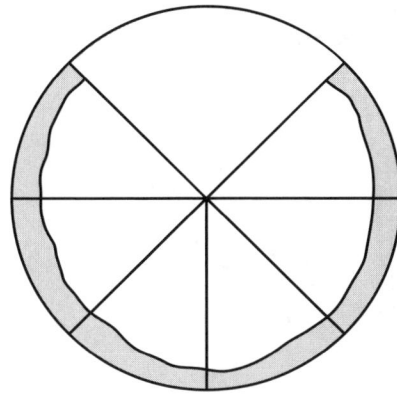 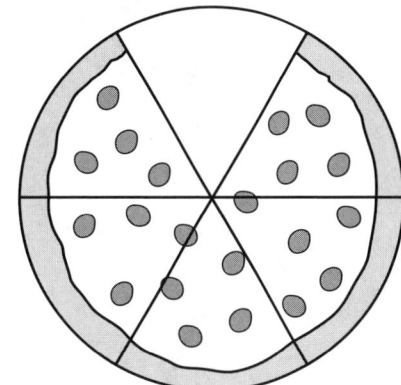

Which of the following statements is **true**?

○ A. Sean ate less pizza than Trevor ate.

○ B. Sean ate more pizza than Trevor ate.

○ C. Trevor ate more pizza than Sean ate.

Go on▶

16 Carolyn is baking a cake. The recipe calls for the amount of milk shown below.

How much milk is Carolyn adding to the cake?

○ A. $1\frac{1}{4}$ cup

○ B. $1\frac{1}{3}$ cup

○ C. $1\frac{1}{2}$ cup

Go on ▶

17 Jonathan and David are sharing a pizza that has been cut into equal-sized pieces.

Jonathan eats some of the pizza.

The picture below shows how much pizza is left.

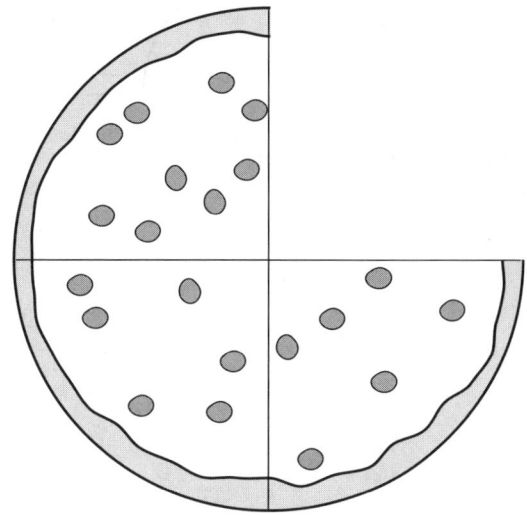

If David eats the same amount as Jonathan, how much of the pizza will be left?

○ **A.** $\frac{1}{4}$

○ **B.** $\frac{1}{3}$

○ **C.** $\frac{1}{2}$

Go on ▶

18 Jamal drew the following shape on a piece of paper in his art class.

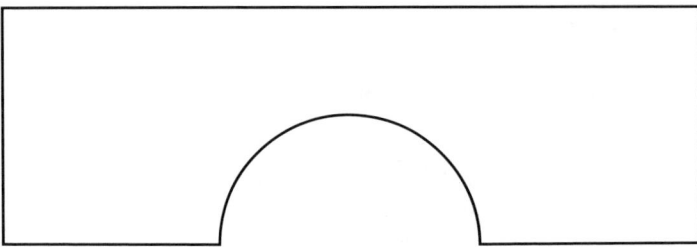

How many **line segments** does this figure have?

○ **A.** 4

○ **B.** 5

○ **C.** 6

Go on ▶

19 Mr. Cavallari drew the following sketch of his sail from his sailboat.

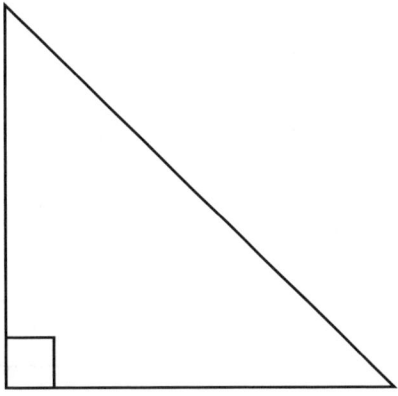

How many **right angles** does this figure have?

○ **A.** 1

○ **B.** 2

○ **C.** 3

Go on ▶

20 Identify the shape below.

☐

Then name **two** properties that define this shape.

21 Using a ruler sketch a rectangle with **two** sides that are 10 cm long and **two** sides that are 4 cm long.

What is the **perimeter** of the rectangle?

Show how you got your answer using words, numbers, or pictures.

What is the perimeter of the rectangle? _____

Go on ▶

22 Roman's garden is in the shape of a rectangle that is 10 feet wide and 15 feet long.

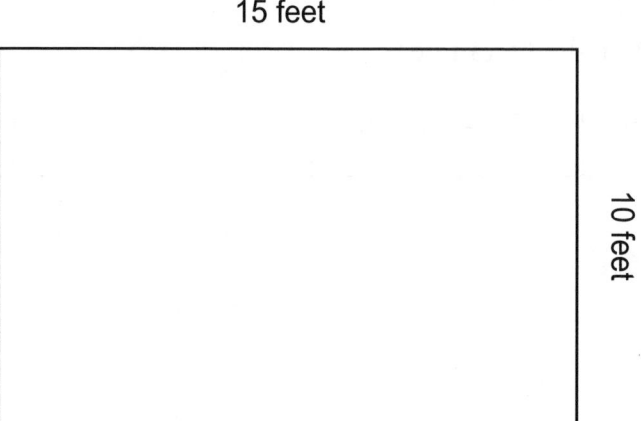

What is the **perimeter** of the garden?

○ **A.** 30 feet

○ **B.** 40 feet

○ **C.** 50 feet

Go on▶

23 Look at the expression below.

$$1 + 8 + 9$$

What expression **equals** the sum?

○ A. $9 + 8 + 2$

○ B. $9 + 1 + 8$

○ C. $1 + 7 + 9$

24 Look at the thermometer shown below.

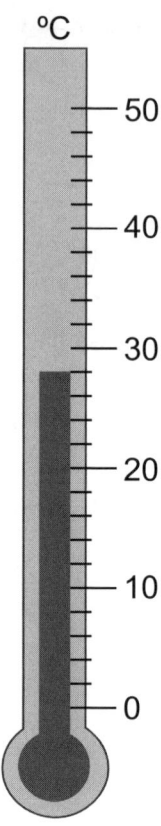

What is the temperature?

○ **A.** 24° C

○ **B.** 28° C

○ **C.** 32° C

Go on ▶

25 Elin was trying to lift a 20-pound tire.

Which of the following is the **approximate** weight of a 20-pound tire?

○ A.   9 kilograms

○ B.   90 kilograms

○ C.   90 grams

26 **About** how much water could a swimming pool hold?

○ A.   20 quarts

○ B.   40 gallons

○ C.   4,000 gallons

Go on ▶

27 Audrey is selling candy bars to help raise money for her school. The bar graph below shows how many candy bars she sold in one week.

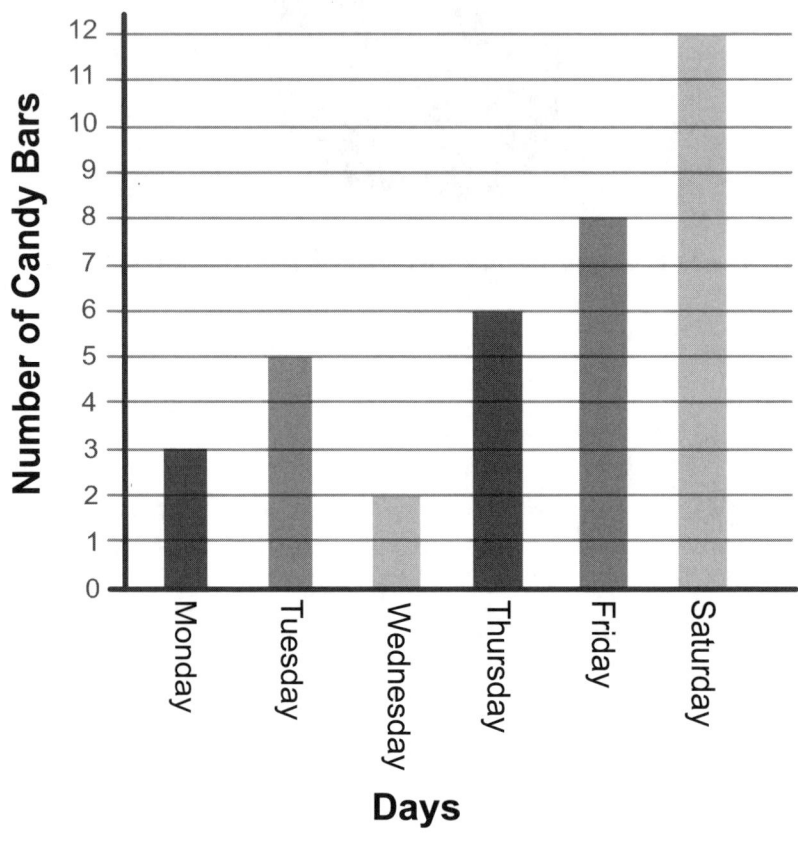

Which of the following statements is **true**?

○ A. Audrey sold twice as many candy bars on Saturday as she did on Thursday.

○ B. Audrey sold three more candy bars on Tuesday than she did on Monday.

○ C. Audrey sold three times as many candy bars on Friday as she did on Wednesday.

Go on ▶

28 Ruth's soccer team played 9 games. Her team scored 7 goals in each of the first 3 games. The team scored 4 goals in each of the last 6 games.

Which shows one way of finding the **total** number of goals the team scored in the 9 games?

○ A. Multiply 7 by 3 by 4 by 6.

○ B. Add 7 and 3. Add 4 and 6. Then multiply the two sums.

○ C. Multiply 7 by 3. Multiply 4 by 6. Then add the two products.

29 Denim City is having sale on jeans. Blue Jeans are on sale for $36.00, Black Jeans are $38.00, and White Jeans are $55.

Jonah bought two pairs Blue Jeans. What information is necessary to know how much Jonah spent on two pairs of Blue Jeans?

○ A. Blue Jeans are $36.00.

○ B. Black Jeans are $38.00.

○ C. White Jeans are $55.00.

Go on ▶

30 Sally is walking to her friends' house that is three blocks away. Sally can walk one block in 10 minutes.

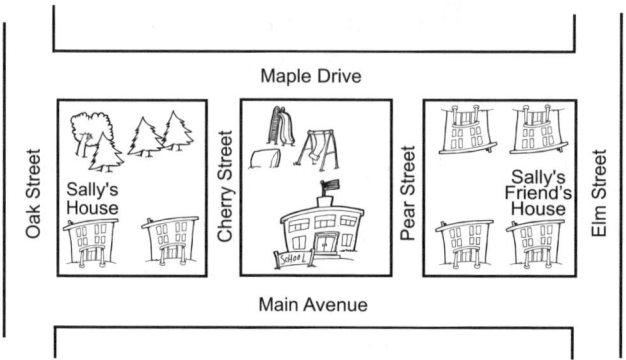

How long will it take Sally get to her friends house? Justify your answer.

Go on ▶

31 The school band is selling t-shirts with "School Spirit" written across the front at the next home basketball game to raise money for new band uniforms.

The band bought 15 boxes of shirts. Each box of shirts cost $25.00 and contains 12 shirts. If the band sold the shirts at $15.00 each, how many shirts would the band need to sell to make their money back?

- A. 20
- B. 25
- C. 30

32 Jason and Will share a newspaper delivery route. Every day, Jason delivers the newspaper to 32 houses and Will delivers the newspaper to 28 houses.

Together, how many newspapers do the boys deliver in one week?

- A. 400
- B. 420
- C. 430

Go on ▶

33 Albert has a model car collection on his shelf. He keeps 14 cars on the top shelf, 6 cars on the middle shelf, and 17 cars on the bottom shelf.

How can Albert find how many cars he has in his collection? Justify your answer.

34 Carmen has 4 cats. Jove weighs 14 pounds. Tate weighs 12 pounds. Whiskers weighs 10 pounds, and Lily weighs 18 pounds. Carmen weighs 100 pounds more than the total weight of the cats.

How many **pounds** does Carmen weigh? Justify your answer.

Go on ▶

35 Mary wants to know about how much her dog Rex weighs, but she doesn't have a scale. She knows that her friend Tara's dog weighs about 40 pounds. Mary decides that Rex also weighs about 40 pounds.

Explain why this may or may not be a good estimate. Use words, numbers, and/or pictures.

Go on ▶

36 The third-grade students at Redwood Elementary School voted for their favorite ice cream flavors. The graph below shows the number of students who voted for each flavor.

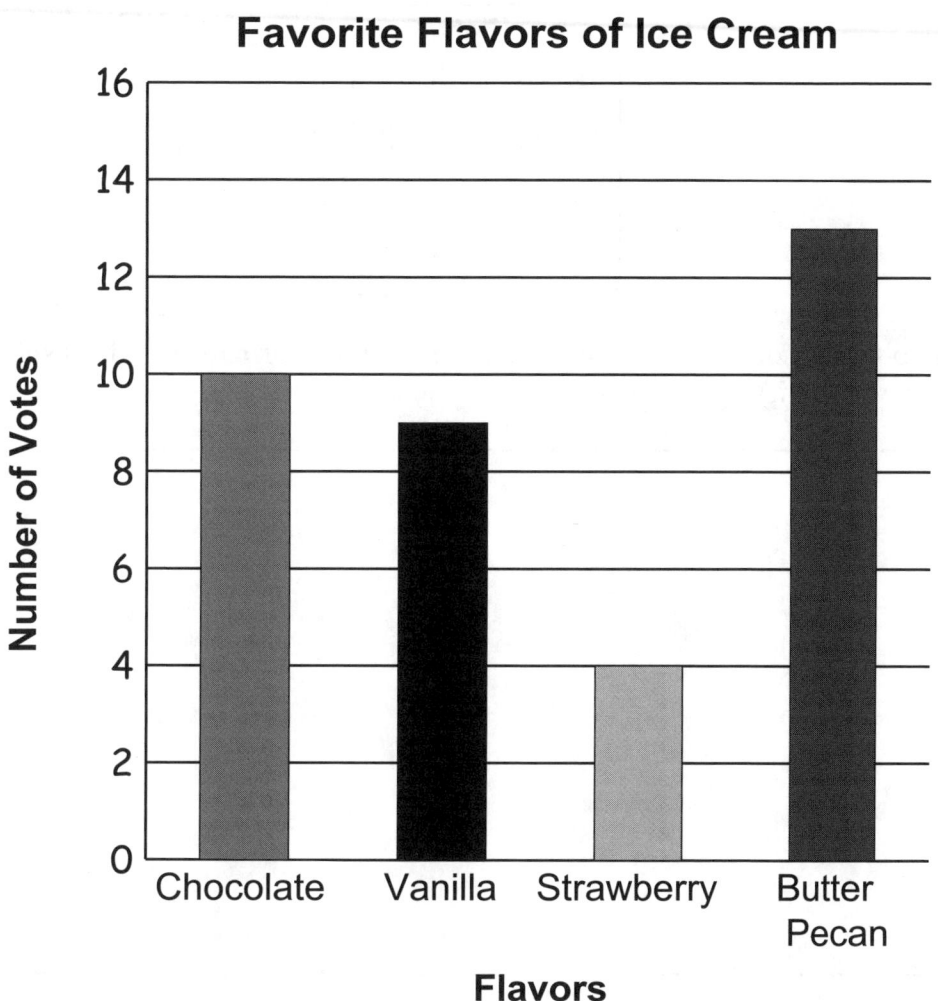

Which flavor will the teachers **most likely** choose to get for the end-of-the-year party?

○ **A.** Vanilla

○ **B.** Strawberry

○ **C.** Butter pecan

Go on ▶

37 Carly takes a survey of her class to find out what pets they have. She makes a tally mark for every pet.

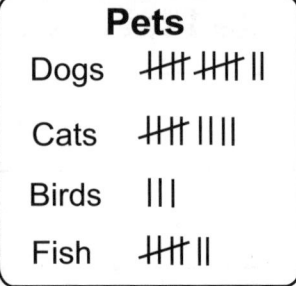

According to Carly's data table, what is the **total** number of cats and dogs she and her classmates have? Justify your answer.

Mathematics Assessment

The Mathematics Assessment is made up of multiple-choice questions, completion items, and short-answer questions. These questions show you how the skills you have learned in Mathematics class may be tested on the Mathematics MSP. The questions also give you a chance to practice your skills. If you have trouble with an area, talk with a parent or teacher.

Read each question carefully. If you do not know an answer, you may skip the question and come back to it later.

When you finish, check your answers.

Directions for Mathematics Assessment

Today you will take the Mathematics Assessment.

Directions to the Student

There are several different types of questions on this Assessment:
1. Some questions will ask you to choose the best answer from three answer choices. These items are worth one point.
2. Some questions will ask you to write your answer in an answer box.
   - Some of these questions are short. They ask you to write only an answer, for example, a single number or one or two words. These items are worth two points.
   - Others ask for more details or more thinking. They ask you to write an answer, to explain your thinking using words, numbers, or pictures, or to show the steps you used to solve a problem. These items are worth two points.

Here are some important things to remember as you take this Assessment:
1. Read each question carefully and think about the answer.
2. If answer choices are given, choose the best answer by filling in the circle in front of your answer.
3. If an answer box is provided, write your answer neatly and clearly **inside** the box and show all your work. Cross out or erase any work you do not want as part of your answer. **Do not use scratch paper.**
4. Use only a **No. 2 pencil,** not a mechanical pencil or pen, to write your answers directly in your test booklet. If you do not have a No. 2 pencil, ask your teacher to give you one.
5. You should have plenty of time to finish every question on the test. If you do not know the answer to a question, go on to the next question. You can come back to that question later.
6. If you finish early, you may check your work in this test section **only**. Do **not** look ahead to the questions in the next sections.
7. When you reach the word **STOP** in your booklet, do not go on until you are told to turn the page.

Go on ▶

1 Which of the following is a **true** number sentence?

○ **A.** 6,987 < 6,897

○ **B.** 7,968 < 6,978

○ **C.** 9,876 > 9,678

2 Chris has a set of 12 dominoes, but some of them are missing.

If he can only find 9 of his dominoes, what fraction represents the number of missing dominoes?

○ **A.** $\frac{1}{9}$

○ **B.** $\frac{3}{12}$

○ **C.** $\frac{4}{12}$

Go on ▶

3 Look at the square below.

Using your ruler, what is the **perimeter** of the square in centimeters? How much **longer** is the perimeter than the length of one side of the square? Show or explain your work using words, numbers, and/or pictures.

The perimeter of the square is _____.

Go on ▶

4 The children in the Clark family record their heights every year on their birthdays.

Clark Children Heights by Age

Age	Trevor	Megan	Bob
4	34 inches	33 inches	36 inches
5	36 inches	35 inches	38 inches
6	38 inches	37 inches	40 inches
7	40 inches	39 inches	42 inches
8	42 inches	41 inches	44 inches
9	44 inches	43 inches	46 inches
10	46 inches	45 inches	48 inches

Using the information in the chart, which of the following is **true**?

○ **A.** When Bob and Megan were the same ages, Bob was never shorter than Megan.

○ **B.** When Megan and Trevor were the same ages, Megan was always taller than Trevor.

○ **C.** When Trevor and Bob were the same ages, Trevor was always taller than Bob.

5 Chen wants to check her answer to this addition problem with estimation.

$$126 + 245 + 283 + 379 = \underline{\quad}$$

She checks her answer by rounding each number to the nearest hundred and then adding.

Which of these choices shows how Chen estimated the sum?

○ **A.** 100 + 200 + 200 + 300 = 800

○ **B.** 100 + 200 + 300 + 400 = 1,000

○ **C.** 100 + 300 + 300 + 400 = 1,100

Go on ▶

6 Virginia spent $3.00 on a notebook and $1.50 on a pen. Lauren wants to know if Virginia will have enough money left to see a movie that costs $4.00.

What does Lauren need to know to figure out if Virginia can go to the movie with her? Justify your answer.

Go on ▶

7 Liza ate one piece of her chocolate chip cookie.

Liza's Cookie

Joshua's Cookie

How many pieces must Joshua eat to **equal** the amount Liza ate?

○ A. $\frac{2}{8}$

○ B. $\frac{4}{8}$

○ C. $\frac{6}{8}$

Go on ▶

8 There are 30 students in Jay's class. Half of the class is going to the zoo on a field trip. They will see the zoo in groups of 5.

How many groups of students will there be? Show or explain your work using words, numbers, and/or pictures.

How many groups of students will there be? _____

Go on ▶

9 Sam has a mug full of hot chocolate.

About how much hot chocolate does a mug hold?

○ **A.**   1 ounce

○ **B.**   1 cup

○ **C.**   1 pint

10 On their way home from their vacation in Wilmington, North Carolina, Anna and her family saw the road sign shown below.

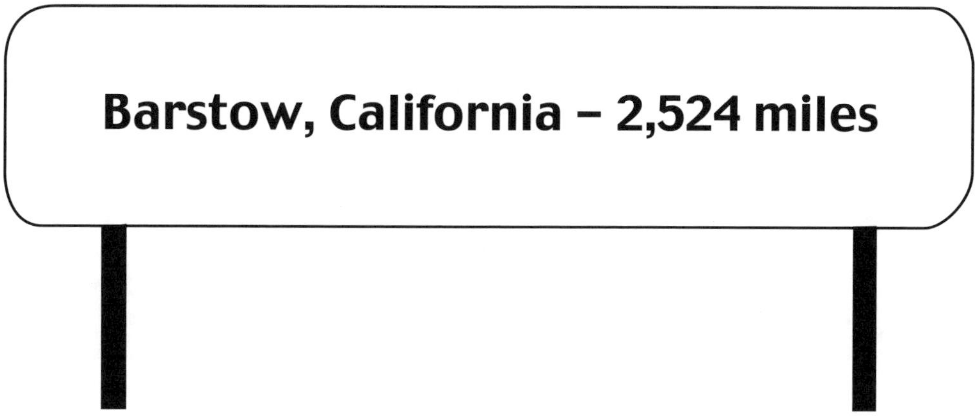

Barstow, California – 2,524 miles

How would this distance be written in word form?

○ **A.**   Twenty-five thousand twenty-four

○ **B.**   Two hundred fifty-two and four tenths

○ **C.**   Two thousand five hundred twenty-four

Go on ▶

11 The wallpaper in Lisa's room has lions on it. On one wall, Lisa counted 39 lions.

- Write about how many lions are on that wall.

> **About how many lions are on that wall?** _____

Go on ▶

12 Max plans on putting a fence around his garden.

6 meters

Max's Garden

5 meters

What is the **perimeter** of the garden? Explain your answer using words and/or pictures.

The perimeter of Max's garden is _____.

Go on ▶

13 There are 4 pots with 3 flowers in each pot.

How many flowers are there in all?

○ **A.** 12

○ **B.** 15

○ **C.** 18

Go on ▶

14 Look at the themometer below.

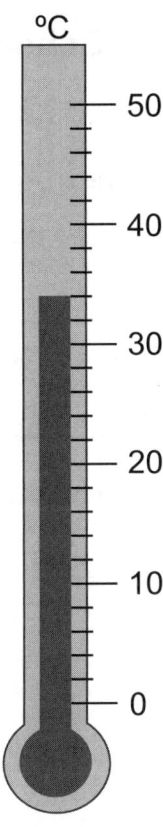

What temperature does the thermometer show?

○ **A.** 32° C

○ **B.** 34° C

○ **C.** 36° C

Go on ▶

15 Look at Louis' tally table below.

Favorite After-School Activities	
Watching TV	IIII
Playing video games	HHT II
Riding bikes	HHT II
Playing with pets	II
Playing a sport	HHT IIII

According to Louis' tally table, how many votes did the most popular after-school activity receive?

○ **A.** 7

○ **B.** 8

○ **C.** 9

Go on ▶

16 In the store, Mr. Walker put out 16 books. He put an equal number of books on each of the 2 shelves.

Which picture shows how he divided the books?

○ **A.**

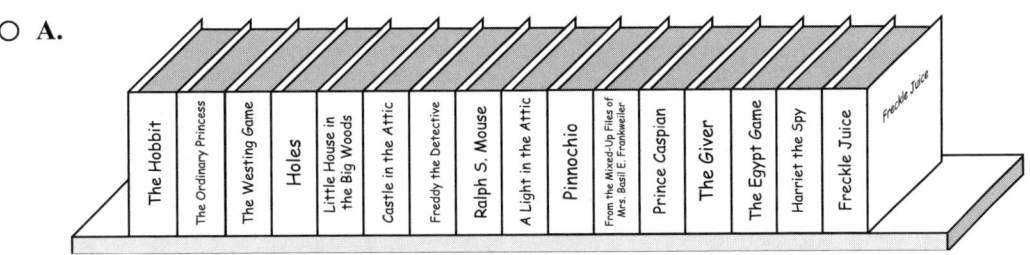

○ **B.**

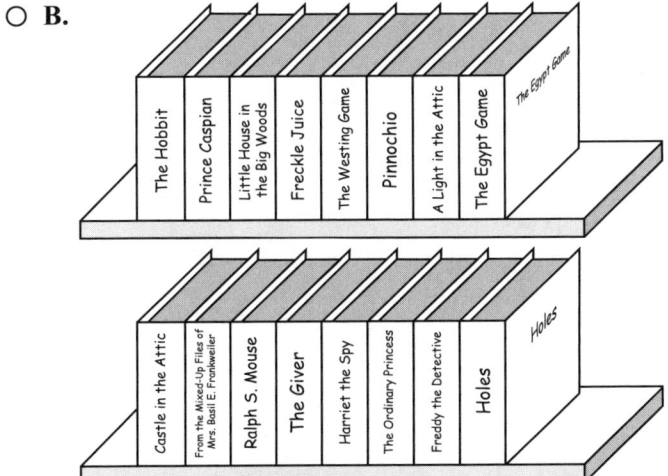

○ **C.**

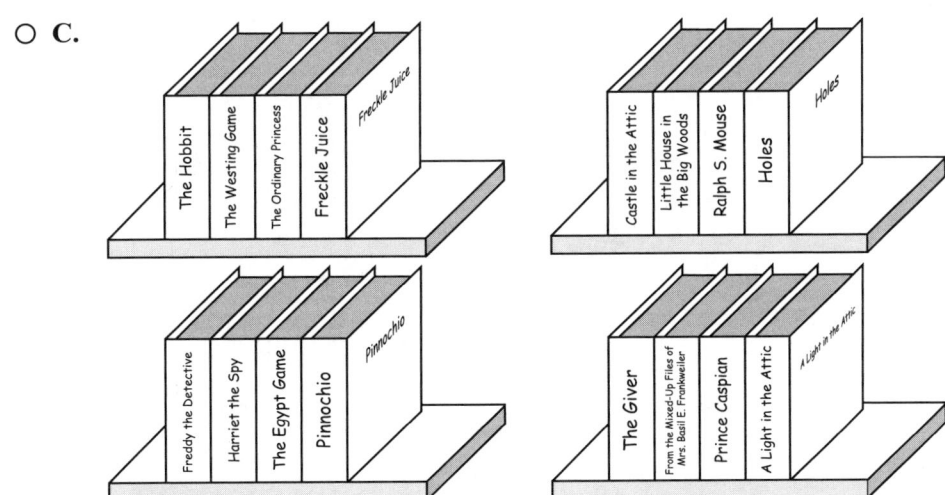

Go on ▶

17 Celia has $18.00. Soft pretzels cost $2.00 each.

How many soft pretzels can Celia buy?

○ A. 8

○ B. 9

○ C. 10

18 A pail holds about

○ A. 3 ounces

○ B. 3 pounds

○ C. 3 gallons

Go on ▶

19 The students in Mr. Sefton's class took a survey to see what holiday was most popular with the students in their class.

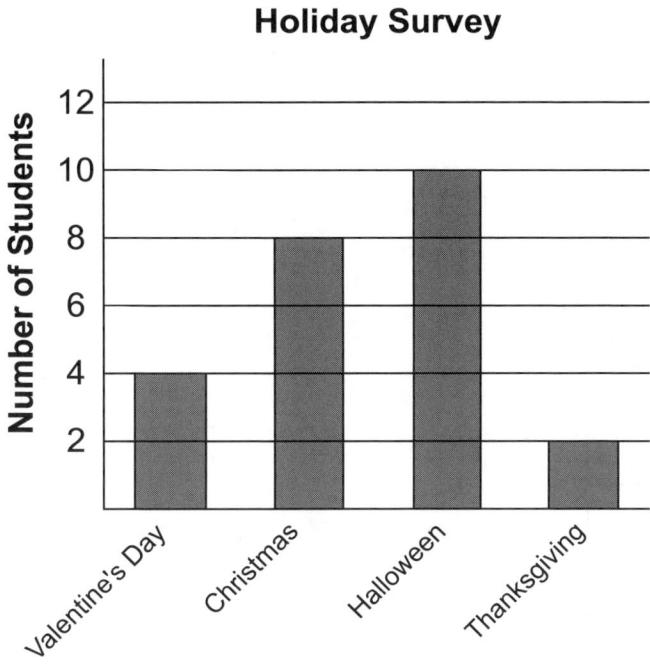

Use the information in the bar graph to find the total number of students in Mr. Sefton's class. Write a number sentence to tell how many students are in Mr. Sefton's class.

Go on ▶

20 Which figure has $\frac{5}{6}$ shaded?

- A.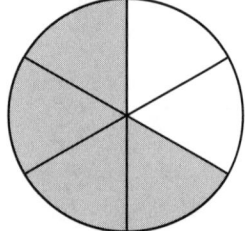

- B.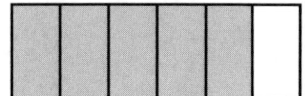

- C.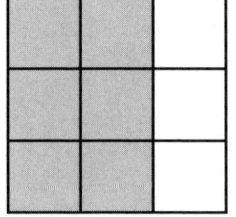

21 Using a ruler, measure the perimeter of the parallelogram. Measure to the nearest centimeter.

What is the perimeter the parallelogram? Show or explain your work using words, numbers, and/or pictures.

Go on ▶

22 Which of these number sentences is **correct**?

○ A. 300 + 40 + 2 = 360

○ B. 400 + 30 + 6 = 409

○ C. 500 + 10 + 2 = 512

Go on ▶

23 Nicole is 6 years old. Nicole's sister Shawna is 5 years older.

Write a number sentence that best represents Shawna's age. Justify your answer.

24 Kevin has 32 model cars and 17 model trucks.

About how many cars and trucks does he have altogether? Estimate to the nearest 10.

○ **A.** 50

○ **B.** 60

○ **C.** 70

Go on ▶

25 Which of the following pairs of lines are parallel to one another?

○ A. | —

○ B. \ /

○ C. | |

26 Bobby drew two circles on the chalkboard for his class to compare.

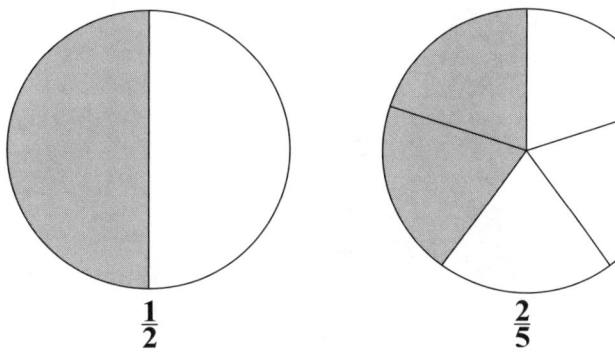

Which of the following is **true** about Bobby's drawings?

○ A. $\frac{1}{2} > \frac{2}{5}$

○ B. $\frac{1}{2} < \frac{2}{5}$

○ C. $\frac{1}{2} = \frac{2}{5}$

Go on ▶

27 Mrs. Garcia has 3 cupcake pans. Each pan has room for 9 cupcakes.

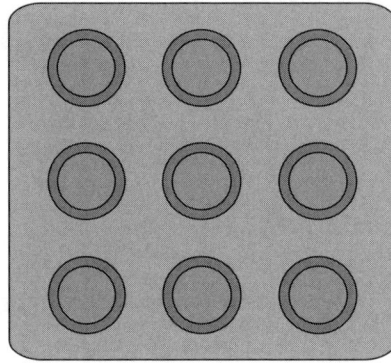

How many cupcakes can Mrs. Garcia bake at one time?

○ **A.** 18 cupcakes

○ **B.** 24 cupcakes

○ **C.** 27 cupcakes

28 Mrs. Goodrich is having a party. She needs 32 servings of lemonade. Each carton of lemonade has about 10 servings in it.

How many cartons should Mrs. Goodrich buy so that she has as many servings as she needs?

○ **A.** 3 cartons

○ **B.** 4 cartons

○ **C.** 10 cartons

Go on ▶

29 Yves walked around the edge of his house. A diagram of Yves' house is shown below.

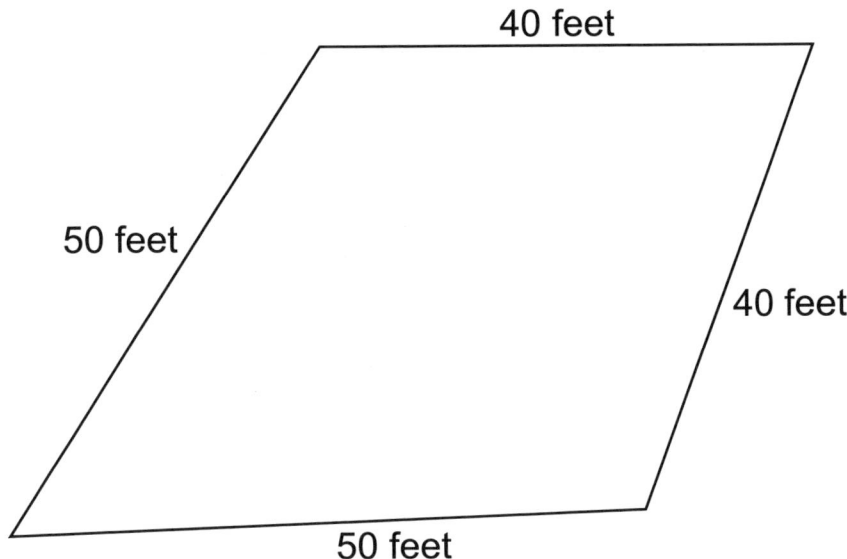

What is the perimeter of his house in feet?

○ **A.** 160 feet

○ **B.** 180 feet

○ **C.** 200 feet

Go on ▶

30 Which number does point Z best represent on the number line below?

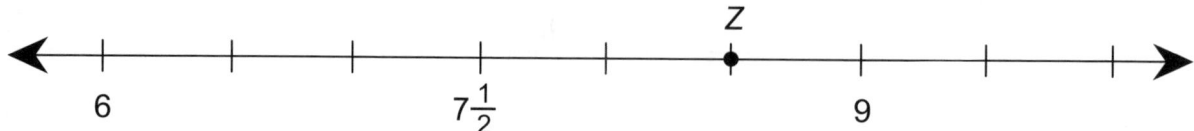

○ A.   7

○ B. $8\frac{1}{2}$

○ C. $9\frac{1}{2}$

Notes

Notes

Notes

Notes

Notes

SHOW WHAT YOU KNOW® ON THE MSP FOR GRADE 3, ADDITIONAL PRODUCTS

Parent/Teacher Supplement
Item #WA1321

Reading Flash Cards
Item #WA5335

Mathematics Flash Cards
Item #WA5332

**For More Information, call our toll-free number: 1.877.PASSING (727.7464)
or visit our website: www.ShowWhatYouKnowPublishing.com**